Beyond Expectations

The Kingdom No One Expected

Charles Garner

Beyond Expectations: *The Kingdom No One Expected*
ISBN: 979-8-9924408-2-9

Copyright© 2025 by Charles Garner and PGS Publishing, LLC

Cover: Titian, *The Crucifixion*, 1555

About the Author

Charles Garner is an author, curriculum designer, and teacher to the church. His B.A. is in Biblical Studies and Social Science. He holds a Master of Religious Education with emphasis in Biblical Exegesis and Theology.

He has authored, edited, or designed over fifty resources and books for use in the Christian community. His works include *Gifts of Grace, Reclaiming the Real Jesus* co-authored with Dr. Ivan Parke, *Thinking of Leaving, A Canary in a Coal Mine* co-authored with Dr. John Powers, *Profiles from Paul*, and *It's NOT Adam's Fault!*.

He and his wife, Nancy, live in the Northern Rockies of Montana.

Table of Contents

Beyond Expectations

The Kingdom No One Expected

1

Unexpected Wine of the Kingdom
The Miracle of His Mission

On the third day, a wedding took place in Cana, a quiet village nestled in the hills of Galilee. Jesus, accompanied by His disciples, and His mother, Mary, were all invited to this celebration. Wine was an essential part of Jewish wedding feasts, a symbol of joy and abundance. Yet, as the celebration wore on, disaster struck—the wine ran out. In the midst of the celebration, Mary, aware of the dilemma, turned to her son. She said simply, *"They have no wine."*

Jesus responded to His mother with what might seem like a cold, distant reply: *"Woman, what does this have to do with me? My hour has not yet come."* It was a response that, at first glance, may seem dismissive or perplexing. But Mary, trusting in Jesus even when His mission had not fully revealed itself, instructed the servants with remarkable confidence, *"Do whatever He tells you."*

Nearby stood six stone water jars, used for the Jewish rites of purification. These vessels, each holding twenty to thirty gallons, were filled with water as part of the purification process, a ritual steeped in tradition. Jesus told the servants, *"Fill the jars with water."* The servants obeyed, filling each jar to the brim.

Then, with a quiet command, He said, *"Draw some out."* The word He used—Ἀντλήσατε (*Antlēsate*)—was not the typical word for drawing or dipping water from a jar. It conveyed the act of drawing water from a deeper source—the well. Jesus was not asking the servants to dip from the purification jars themselves, but rather to use the water jug—the seventh vessel—to draw more water from the well. As they did, the water in that jug was miraculously transformed into the finest wine.

9

The master of the feast, tasting the wine, marveled at the quality. He called the bridegroom over, astonished, saying, *"Everyone serves the good wine first, and when people have drunk freely, then the poor wine. But you have kept the good wine until now."*

This moment marked the first of Jesus' signs, and it was not merely a miracle of convenience; it was a revelation of His mission. Jesus had not just provided a solution to a logistical problem, but had revealed the deeper reality of what He was bringing into the world—a new era, a new covenant, a Kingdom that would overflow with grace, joy, and life. The old had passed away. In its place, Jesus was ushering in something far better—fresh, new, and life-giving.

Through this act, Jesus demonstrated that He was not just fulfilling the Law of purification, but transcending it. Bringing about a new kind of cleansing, one that would be rooted in grace, not ritual. He had come to bring *new wine*, the wine of the Kingdom of God.

"Unexpected Wine"
In Cana, where joy filled the air,
Feast of promise, bride and groom, joyful pair
But the wine ran dry, and joy stood still—
A quiet problem with no will to fill.
Then Mary spoke with quiet grace,
Her faith in Him lit up the place:
"They have no wine, my son—do care."
A humble plea, beyond despair.
With words so gentle, yet full of might,
"Woman, my time has not come to light."
But faith knew better, His heart was near,
She whispered to servants, "Do not fear."
Six jars, for purity's old ways,
Filling the day with ritual praise,
Jesus spoke to fill them full,
Water drawn, a cleansing rule.

But He, the Master, had come to bring,
Something deeper, a new kind of spring.
"Draw once more," He told them so,
And the water turned to finest flow.
The master tasted, amazed at the gift,
The finest wine, a holy lift.
"Why save the best, when all is done?"
But the Kingdom's joy had just begun.
The old was gone, the new had come,
In Jesus' hands, the work was done.
From water to wine, He made it clear,
The Kingdom of God is drawing near.

The Miracle at Cana is profound on several levels. First, it reveals the nature of Jesus' mission in a way that would have been shocking to His contemporaries. The traditional Jewish rites of purification were an important part of their religious and cultural identity, but these rites could only go so far. They were symbols of cleansing, but they were incomplete. The six stone jars, filled with water, represent the incomplete and insufficient nature of the Law—good, but lacking the ability to truly transform the heart.

By choosing these six jars—each holding 20-30 gallons—and commanding them to be filled to the brim with water, Jesus did not nullify the Law; rather, He fulfilled it in a way that was unexpected. He did not come to abolish the Law (Matthew 5:17), but to complete it. In Jewish symbolism, the number six often conveyed a sense of incompletion, especially in contrast to the number seven, which symbolized divine completeness.

The seventh vessel, by which the water was drawn from the well, represents Jesus Himself—the fulfillment of all that the Law pointed toward. Through His ministry, He would bring the completion of God's plan, ushering in a new era where the Law would be written on the hearts of His people, not merely in external rituals.

Furthermore, the transformation of water into wine speaks volumes about the nature of the Kingdom Jesus was establishing. Wine, in Jewish tradition, was a symbol of joy, celebration, and abundance. To save the best wine for last, after all guests had already had their fill, was a striking contrast to human expectations. In the Kingdom of God, the best is reserved for the end—the fulfillment of joy, peace, and eternal life, which Jesus would bring to fruition through His death and resurrection.

The miracle also highlights the nature of the new covenant: the Law offered temporary purification, Jesus offers lasting transformation. The Law could not provide what was truly needed—lasting change of the heart and eternal fellowship with God. The new wine, then, a symbol of the new way of relating to God that Jesus came to bring—grace, joy, and eternal life only He could offer.

This miracle is both an introduction to Jesus' ministry and a foreshadowing of the Kingdom He came to establish. Through simple obedience—filling the jars to the brim, drawing from the deep vessel—the servants became participants in the miraculous, just as we, too, are invited to participate in the miraculous work of God in our lives. What was once ordinary—water—became extraordinary. What was once incomplete—the old ways of purification—became complete in Christ. Through Jesus, the best was yet to come.

Reflections

1. What does the miracle at Cana reveal about the character of Jesus and the nature of His Kingdom?

2. Why do you think Jesus, in a quiet, almost hidden moment, performed His first miracle (John's first sign in his Gospel)?

3. How does the transformation of water into wine challenge our assumptions about divine intervention?

4. In what areas of your life are you still trying to find joy from the old jars, when Jesus is offering you the new wine of the Kingdom?

Introduction

You've already read the first vignette—and that wasn't a mistake.

The miracle at the wedding in Cana—the turning of water into wine—was not only the first sign of Jesus' public ministry, it also sets the tone for everything that follows. Quiet, almost unnoticed, and tucked away at a small celebration in Galilee, this moment revealed far more than the transformation of water into wine. It revealed the character of the Kingdom to come.

At first glance, this miracle may seem simple, even incidental. But it is far more than that. It is the first glimpse of a Kingdom that does not announce itself with spectacle or domination, but with quiet grace. The water from a well becomes the finest wine of joy and abundance. What had run out is renewed—not through effort, but through the presence of the King. Those at the wedding were surprised by the deed and the quality of the wine. And just as they were surprised, throughout His entire ministry, Jesus consistently defied expectations.

This book invites you on a journey through that surprising Kingdom. Jesus came not to validate assumptions, but to redefine them. What He brought into the world was not grounded in wealth, politics, or visible authority, but in the quiet revolution of the Spirit working through a Servant-King. From the very outset, Jesus revealed a Kingdom that would not conform to human imagination—it would transform it.

The Old Testament is filled with prophecies about a coming Messiah—a deliverer who would restore justice, defeat Israel's enemies, and establish God's reign. These promises shaped the Jewish people's hopes, especially during the Roman occupation, when the longing for liberation burned hot. They expected a warrior. A king. A conqueror.

What they received was something altogether different.

Jesus came not to seize power, but to surrender Himself. Not to build an earthly empire, but to call people into a Kingdom not of this world. His mission transcended borders and thrones. And because He didn't fit the mold, many rejected Him. Even His closest followers struggled to understand who He really was.

And yet, Jesus' every word, every act, every step He took revealed the truth: the Kingdom had come.

This book traces that unfolding through a series of vignettes—moments in the life of Jesus that illuminate the surprising nature of the Kingdom He preached. We will not attempt to cover every event in His ministry. Rather, we will focus on the signs, events, exchanges, confrontations, teachings—that reveal the essence of His mission and message. Each vignette ends with reflection questions for personal insight or group Bible study use.

These moments will take us from unexpected joy at a wedding feast to the agony of Gethsemane...from a boat on a stormy sea to a table filled with sinners...from the hush of a hillside sermon to the echoing rumble of an empty tomb. Along the way, we will see again and again that Jesus did not come to meet our expectations—He came to exceed them.

The Kingdom of God was, and still is, beyond what we imagine. It confronts us. It invites us. It reshapes how we see power, love, purpose, and even death.

These pages are not just a study. They are an invitation—to see the King, and to step into His Kingdom...a Kingdom not of might, but of mercy. A Kingdom not made by human hands, but written into the fabric of eternity. A Kingdom that still comes quietly...like water changed to wine.

2

The Purpose of God
Forming a People for Himself

From the very beginning, God's intent was clear: He desired to create a people for Himself. Genesis 1:26-27 reveals this profound truth: *Let us make man in our image, after our likeness…*. Humanity was created to reflect God's glory, to share in His divine fellowship, and to enjoy relationship with Him. God didn't need people, but He chose to create them out of His will and desire. In His self-sufficiency, He longed to share His glory with others.

This divine plan for a people began in the Garden of Eden. Yet, humanity's first act was one of rebellion. Adam and Eve disobeyed God by eating from the forbidden tree, and thus sin entered the world. The choice to disobey would become the tragic pattern repeated by every human being, except for Jesus. However, God did not abandon His purpose. In His infinite mercy, He had already established a plan for redemption through Jesus Christ.

Even before the world was made, God had predestined a people for Himself, as Paul reminds us in Ephesians 1:3–10. God's plan of redemption was always through Jesus—the Lamb slain before time. Even in the face of human rebellion, God's promise remained, and the path to reconciliation would be through the sacrifice of His Son.

The crucifixion of Jesus is the fulfillment of this eternal plan. Jesus, fully God and fully man, perfectly obeyed the Father in every way. His death on the cross was the sacrificial payment for humanity's sin. This act of obedience was the completion of God's plan to create a people who would be His own possession (1 Peter 2:9-10). Through Jesus' sacrifice, God reconciled the world to Himself, offering forgiveness to all who would receive it by faith.

The church, the *ekklesia*, is this called-out people, chosen to proclaim the excellencies of God, who called them out of darkness into His marvelous light. The gospel declares that God has always had one plan—to form a people for Himself. The resurrection of Jesus sealed the victory of God's Kingdom, now unfolding on earth as a present reality, while we await its ultimate fulfillment.

Through the death and resurrection of Jesus, God is reconciling all things to Himself. This is the story that shapes our identity: creation, rebellion, and redemption. As we live as part of God's Kingdom, we are called to partner with Him in sharing this good news, spreading the message of reconciliation to the world.

"The Purpose Fulfilled"
In the beginning, God declared,
"Let us make man, in our image shared."
A people to reflect His light,
To walk in fellowship, pure and bright.
But in the garden, sin began,
A choice made by the first of man.
Rebellion marked the human way,
Yet God prepared another way.
For in the fullness of all time,
God sent His Son to heal the crime.
Through Jesus' death upon the tree,
That we might be truly free.
The cross, the throne of kingship found,
A sacrificial love unbound.
Now, in Christ, we are made new,
A chosen people, born anew.
With faith in Him, we rise and stand,
Redeemed, adopted by His hand.
To share the news, the Kingdom call,
A people gathered, one and all.

The narrative of God's creation of humanity in His image (Gen. 1:26 -27) sets the foundation for understanding the central theme of God's desire for a people who belong to Him. This concept is not new, but rather embedded in the very fabric of Scripture. From the beginning, God intended for humanity to reflect His glory and participate in His divine fellowship.

This divine image, however, was marred by sin. Humanity's rebellion in the Garden of Eden was not a surprise to God; He had already foreseen it. And within this divine foresight, He initiated a plan for redemption. The Apostles, especially Paul, spoke of this in Ephesians 1, where God's purpose to create a people for Himself, a holy nation, was predestined in Christ. This was not an afterthought, but part of God's eternal design.

At the heart of redemption lies the person and work of Jesus Christ. As a fully divine and fully human figure, Jesus lived a perfect life, obeying the Father's will even unto death (Phil. 2:8). His death on the cross was not only a fulfillment of prophecy but also the ultimate expression of God's love and justice. As Paul explains in Romans 3:21-26, the death of Jesus served to satisfy God's holiness and justice while simultaneously displaying His mercy and grace.

Through Jesus, God offered humanity reconciliation. The cross becomes the point at which God's justice and mercy meet. Through His sacrifice, God reconciled the world to Himself, offering forgiveness to all who place their faith in Jesus (2 Corinthians 5:16-21).

The church, or the *ekklesia*, is the people God has called out of darkness into His marvelous light (1 Peter 2:9-10). This people is not just a future reality but a present one. The Kingdom of God, inaugurated through the death and resurrection of Jesus, is already in motion, and those who are part of it are called to partner with God in spreading the message of reconciliation to the world. The church's mission, then, is to make disciples, sharing the good news of Jesus Christ, and pointing to the fullness of God's Kingdom.

As followers of Jesus, we are part of this grand story of redemption. God has formed a people for Himself, and that includes us. We have been called out of darkness and into the light of His Kingdom. This truth has profound implications for our lives. First, it compels us to live in light of our new identity as God's chosen people, reflecting His glory in everything we do. Secondly, it calls us to be active participants in God's mission of reconciliation. We are ambassadors for Christ, entrusted with the message of the gospel (2 Cor. 5:18-20).

Our partnership with God in spreading the good news is not optional—it is a fundamental part of being in His Kingdom. The story of creation, rebellion, and redemption is the story that defines us. And our mission is clear: to declare this story to a world in need of the reconciliation that comes through Jesus Christ. As we live out this mission, we are fulfilling God's eternal purpose of creating a people for Himself, a people who will bring glory to His name both now and forever.

Let us boldly proclaim the good news that Jesus has died and risen to reconcile the world to God, inviting others into the same reconciliation we have received. In doing so, we fulfill God's eternal intent and live as part of His Kingdom, now and in the age to come.

Reflections

1. How does understanding that God created humanity to share in His glory and fellowship shape your sense of identity?
2. What does it mean that God's plan for redemption through Jesus existed before creation? How does this influence how you view your relationship with God?
3. In what ways do you see the church today reflecting the calling of being "a people for God's own possession"? Where do you feel we fall short?
4. How does your role as an ambassador for Christ influence your relationships, priorities, or daily choices?

3

The Hand of Providence
God's Sovereign Choice in Abraham

The unfolding of God's plan to form a people for Himself is not merely a series of disconnected events but a carefully woven tapestry of divine providence. God's sovereign hand directs all aspects of human history, from the smallest of decisions to the grandest of kingdoms, all in pursuit of His eternal purpose: to call out a people for His name. This thread of providence runs through the lives of His chosen servants, who, whether in times of triumph or trial, are instruments of His will.

Take for example Abram. God's calling of Abram was a sovereign choice—God's decision to create a covenant relationship with him was not based on Abram's merit or goodness, but on God's grace and purpose. In Genesis 12:1-3, God promises to make of Abram a great nation, a blessing to the nations of the earth. Through Abram's lineage, God would ultimately bring forth the Savior of the world. This calling was not an arbitrary choice. God set aside Abram, a man from a pagan lineage, to be the father of a people that would one day reflect His glory to the world.

God's providence is also starkly seen in the life of Joseph, one of Abram's descendants. Sold into slavery by his own brothers, wrongfully accused of a crime, and forgotten by those he helped, Joseph's life seemed to be a series of unfortunate events. Yet, at the pinnacle of his story, he could look back and say, *"You meant evil against me, but God meant it for good"* (Genesis 50:20). This was providence at work—God taking human evil and turning it toward His sovereign purposes. Joseph's position in Egypt would eventually save the entire nation of Israel from famine, thus preserving the chosen people from destruction.

Moses was another man whose life was marked by providence. His preservation as a baby in the bulrushes of the Nile, the adoption by Pharaoh's daughter, and his training in the courts of Egypt were all part of God's plan to raise him up as the deliverer of Israel. Even the act of killing the Egyptian taskmaster and fleeing to Midian was part of God's divine shaping of Moses. There, in the wilderness, he learned humility, leadership, and the shepherding of sheep—skills he would need to shepherd God's people. God's call from the burning bush was the culmination of His providence in Moses' life, and through him, God would reveal His power and faithfulness to His people.

David's anointing as king provides another example of divine providence. When the prophet Samuel came to anoint the next king of Israel, the most obvious candidate—the eldest son of Jesse—was passed over. Instead, God chose David, the youngest and most unlikely of the brothers, to be king. This was the man after God's own heart, through whom the Messiah would come. God's hand of providence was visible in every step of David's life, including his triumph over Goliath, his kingship, and his role in establishing a kingdom through which the line of the Messiah would ultimately be fulfilled.

The inclusion of Rahab and Ruth in the lineage of Jesus further illustrates God's providence. Rahab, a Canaanite prostitute, was saved by her faith in the God of Israel and became an ancestor of King David (Matthew 1:5). Ruth, a Moabite widow and David's great-grandmother, was also part of that same redemptive line through which Jesus would one day be born. These unlikely women, whose lives were marked by loss and exile, were included in the genealogy of the Savior—a testimony to the fact that God's purpose is not limited by human expectation or social boundaries.

Even in the Babylonian Exile, when God's people were taken captive, God's providence was at work. Babylon, unlike the Assyrians before them, chose not to assimilate conquered peoples but allowed them to maintain their identities. This would set the stage for the development of the synagogue, a key institution for the Jewish people during the exile, and later an essential base for the early Christian church. The exiled Jews maintained their identity in foreign lands, preparing the way for the spread of the gospel.

Moreover, the rise of Cyrus, the Persian king who would eventually overthrow Babylon and permit the Jews to return to their land and rebuild their temple, was itself a providential act. In Isaiah 45:1, God calls Cyrus His "anointed"—a title reserved for Israel's kings—long before he ever arose to power. God's providence both preserved His people and prepared their return to the land promised to their forefathers.

From the call of Abram to return from exile, from the story of Joseph to the anointing of David, God's hand was moving the pieces of history into place to fulfill His eternal plan: to create a people for Himself. Throughout all of human history, God is at work in the glove of human events, moving history forward toward His goal—the establishment of His Kingdom and the redemption of a people.

"Providence Unseen"
In quiet hands, the world does turn,
Where unseen forces twist and burn;
A child in reeds, a cry in air,
Providence whispers everywhere.
From favored son to purchased slave,
Put in place—a world to save.
A slave to kings, a king to slaves,
The hand of God makes a way.
A shepherd's heart, a throne prepared,
In humble steps, a kingdom shared.
Through Rahab's faith, through Ruth's lament,
The Savior's line—God's will defined

From exile's chains to walls rebuilt,
God's hand is firm, His plan fulfilled.
The nations rise, the nations fall,
But His good plan will crown them all.
So trust the path where we may tread,
His sovereign will, our daily bread.
The story ends as it began—
A people saved by sovereign plan.

The concept of providence ties these biblical narratives together, illustrating God's active, unseen role in guiding history. Providence is not passive; it is God's constant engagement with His creation, ensuring that His purposes come to fruition. The lives of Abram, Joseph, Moses, David, and others show that God's sovereign will moves through human decisions, even those motivated by evil or rebellion, to accomplish His greater plan.

This theme of providence also explains how God's people could thrive despite seemingly disastrous circumstances. Whether in Egypt, in Babylon, or in the wilderness, God's hand was behind the scenes, shaping events to prepare His people for their role in redemptive history. The Babylonian exile, for instance, though painful, proved to be a strategic moment for God's people, as it helped solidify their identity and set the stage for the eventual return to the land and the rebuilding of the temple. Even the rise of Cyrus was an act of divine sovereignty, fulfilling God's promise to bring His people back to their land. Thus, what seemed like a season of loss became a foundation for future restoration.

In the broader biblical narrative, this providential guidance is also evident in God's overarching plan to establish a kingdom—first in Israel, then through the church, and ultimately in the new heaven and new earth. The lineage of Jesus, which includes unexpected figures like Rahab and Ruth, serves as a powerful reminder that God's providence is not constrained by human expectations or societal norms. He works through the unlikely and the outcast, weaving them into His redemptive story.

As Christians, we are called to trust in God's providential hand in our own lives. While we may not always see or understand how God is working, we can take comfort in the fact that He is sovereign over all things. From the painful seasons of our lives to the joyous victories, God is guiding us toward His purpose.

This should inspire us to live with confidence and hope, knowing that God is actively at work in our world today. Whether in our personal lives, our communities, or on the global stage, God's providence assures us that He is moving history toward its final culmination—the return of Jesus and the establishment of God's eternal kingdom. As we live our lives and share the gospel, we join in this grand, providential story, trusting that our efforts are part of God's sovereign plan to redeem a people for Himself.

In times of uncertainty, we must remember: God's hand is in the glove of human events, shaping history for His glory and the good of His people. Nothing happens by chance.

Reflections

1. How does God's choice of unexpected people (like Abram, Rahab, and Ruth) shape your understanding of who He can use in His purposes today?

2. Joseph said, *"You meant evil against me, but God meant it for good."* How does this truth speak into the difficult or painful seasons of your own life?

3. The Babylonian Exile felt like a defeat but prepared the people for restoration. Can you think of a time in your life when loss became the groundwork for future growth?

4. What does it look like to live with trust in God's providence in a world that often feels chaotic or uncertain?

What Is the Kingdom of God?

Throughout this book, we explore the phrase *"the Kingdom of God."* Scripture presents the Kingdom of God in three distinct ways:

1. Where God is King: *"The kingdom is the Lord's, and He rules over the nations* (Ps. 22:28)." God reigns in sovereignty—past, present, or future. He is King by virtue of creation (Ps. 24).

2. When God's reign is fully revealed: Jesus spoke of a coming Kingdom at the end of the age (Mark 14:25). Paul stated: *"Then comes the end, when He delivers the Kingdom to God the Father* (1 Corinthians 15:24)." This is the Kingdom in its end-time, final, glorious fulfillment—when every wrong is made right.

3. Whom God rules: *"The Kingdom of God is in your midst* (Luke 17:21)." Jesus taught that the Kingdom begins now. Jesus told a scribe who defined the greatest commandment that he was near to allowing God to rule his life (Mark 12:34). Whomever and wherever God's will is done in the lives of His people, He reigns.

The Kingdom of God is the dynamic reign of God—across time and realms and within the lives of individuals. In the person of Jesus the Christ, the Kingdom of God—God's redemptive reign—broke into human history in a unique and decisive way. God's rule was revealed not as political power, but as a redemptive, personal, and cosmic reality. It is "already—and not yet"—both a realized presence and a future promise.

Journaling: Living Under the King
1. With which aspect of God's Kingdom are you most familiar—His cosmic reign, His end-time kingdom, or His rule in your own heart?
2. How do you experience God's reign in your daily life?
3. Are there places in your life where you resist His kingship?
4. What would it look like to surrender more fully to His rule?

4

Orchestrating Nations
God's Sovereignty Over the Nations

Let's begin by considering the concept of time and timing, particularly as Paul describes it in Galatians 4:4-5: *But when the fullness of time had come, God sent forth His Son, born of woman, born under the law, to redeem those who were under the law, so that we might receive adoption as sons.* Here, Paul speaks of a divinely orchestrated moment, when the time was "right" for the arrival of Jesus, both to accomplish the redemption of humanity and to establish the Kingdom of God. This perfect timing aligns with the larger narrative of history, which God governs sovereignly, as seen in passages like Acts 17:26 and Daniel 2.

God's sovereignty over history includes His orchestration of the rise and fall of nations, each serving His divine purposes. As the psalmist declares, *For kingship belongs to the Lord, and he rules over the nations* (Psalm 22:28). And as Job wisely affirms, *He makes the nations great, then destroys them; He enlarges the nations, then leads them away* (Job 12:23). In Acts 17:26, we are reminded that God *determined their appointed times and the boundaries of their habitation.* Through this sovereignty, He fulfills His eternal plan—both for Israel and the broader world.

God's orchestration of history is evident in the rise and fall of empires. For instance, He used the Assyrians to punish Israel's northern tribes for their idolatry and disobedience. The Assyrians' policy of dispersion and absorption left the "Ten Lost Tribes" scattered. However, this judgment was part of God's broader redemptive plan for Israel, and once His purpose was served, the Assyrians were no longer needed.

25

In contrast, the Babylonian Empire played a different role in God's plan. It was raised to discipline the Southern Kingdom of Judah, not by dispersing the people but by exiling them, yet maintaining their cultural identity. This enabled Judah to survive and later return to its land. The Babylonian Empire only lasted long enough to fulfill God's purpose and was replaced by the Medo-Persian Empire, which would continue His work of restoring His people.

The Medo-Persian Empire was a key instrument in God's plan for the Jews. Cyrus, the Persian king, was specifically chosen by God to end the Jewish exile and support their return to Jerusalem. In Isaiah 44:28, God calls Cyrus by name 176 years before he fulfilled his mission, showing that God orchestrates all events in history to bring about His will.

At the center of these divine plans is the interpretation given to a young man named Daniel—a key that unlocks the mysteries of history. The Babylonian king, Nebuchadnezzar, had a dream in which he saw a massive and terrifying statue of a man made of various metals. The head was gold, the chest and arms were of silver, the stomach and thighs were of bronze, the legs and feet were of iron with the feet a mixture of iron and clay. Daniel, a young exiled Jew was given the interpretation of the dream for the king. What God revealed to Daniel was profound and far-reaching.

The statue's parts represented different kingdoms and the dream spanned centuries of history.

- Gold: Representing the Babylonian Empire (612–539 B.C.)
- Silver: Representing the Medo-Persian Empire (539–331 B.C.)
- Bronze: Representing the Greek Empire (331–146 B.C.)
- Iron and Clay: Representing the Roman Empire (63 B.C.–A.D. 1453)

Ultimately, however, a stone strikes the statue, shattering it and becoming a mountain that fills the whole earth—representing God's eternal Kingdom, which will outlast all earthly empires.

This dream was a prophecy of God's sovereignty over history, showing that while earthly kingdoms rise and fall, His kingdom would ultimately stand forever, surpassing all other powers. A kingdom that would never end, ruling over all the kingdoms of the earth. This dream was a prophecy of God's sovereignty over history, showing that while earthly kingdoms rise and fall, His kingdom would ultimately stand forever, surpassing all other powers. Let's explore this dream and its meaning.

Segment 1: The Sovereignty of God in History

God's transcendence over human history is a foundational truth in Scripture. He orchestrates the rise and fall of kingdoms to fulfill His purposes. From Psalm 22:28 to Acts 17:26, we see that God is not passive in history; He actively governs the events of nations to bring about His divine plan.

Exploring specific empires God raised up, we see that each one contributed to the *"fullness of time"* in ways that prepared the world for the arrival of Jesus. This timing was not chance but God's careful orchestration. God raised up each kingdom and empire, allowing them to fulfill His redemptive purposes in the unfolding of history.

"Sovereign Over Nations"

The nations rise, the kingdoms fall,
God's hand is present, ruling all.
From Babel's tower to Rome's vast height,
His purpose moves, His plan takes flight.
Kings may come, and empires fade,
God's decree does not give way.
In history's flow, His will still stands,
His timing works by His own hand.

The verses from Psalm 22:28, Job 12:23, Acts 17:26, and Daniel 2:21 affirm the idea that God is in control of the nations and history.

He raises up kings and empires, and He also brings them down, all according to His sovereign will.

The *"fullness of time"* refers to the idea that God has a set moment in history for certain events to unfold. The birth of Jesus was not an accident; it occurred at a time when the groundwork of the empires that came before had prepared the world for the spread of His message. The right time had come for the gospel to be proclaimed and received by the nations.

Segment 2: The Persian Empire's Contribution

The Persian Empire (539-331 B.C.) played a significant role in shaping the time before Christ. Under King Cyrus, the Persians allowed the Jewish people to return to their land after the Babylonian exile and even supported the rebuilding of the Temple in Jerusalem. This marked a moment of hope and restoration for the Jewish people, a pivotal step in God's plan of redemption.

Additionally, the Persians established a postal system that allowed for faster communication and travel across the vast empire. This system laid the groundwork for the rapid spread of ideas and news—a crucial factor for the spread of the gospel after Jesus' resurrection. God's sovereign orchestration is evident in how He used this empire to prepare the world for His greater plan.

"Anointed by God"

Cyrus, the shepherd, brought release,
To God's people, bringing peace.
A road for letters, swift and wide,
To carry news to every side.
From East to West, from sea to shore,
The message spread, forever more.
God used the Persian hand to show,
His plan for Christ would soon unfold.

28

- Restoration of the Jews: The Persian Empire's support of the Jewish return to their land set the stage for the eventual birth of Jesus in Bethlehem. It allowed for the continuity of Jewish identity and faith, which would become the foundation for the spread of Christianity. As Isaiah 44:28 prophesied, Cyrus was called by God to rebuild Jerusalem, and this restoration was crucial for God's redemptive plan.

- The Persian Postal System: The postal system introduced by the Persians allowed communication across vast distances to become more efficient. This post system would prove invaluable for the spread of the message of Jesus throughout the Roman Empire. As Acts 17:26-27 reminds us, God *"determined their appointed times and the boundaries of their habitation,"* even orchestrating systems like this to fulfill His purposes.

Segment 3: The Greek Empire's Contribution

The Greek Empire, under Alexander the Great, spread Greek culture, language, and ideas throughout much of the known world (331-146 B.C.). This cultural expansion, called Hellenization, meant that many regions, including Palestine, adopted Greek as a common language. This linguistic unity facilitated the gospel's spread, as the message could now be communicated widely in a common tongue.

Additionally, the philosophical environment created by Greek thought helped prepare people to understand concepts of the divine, morality, and the nature of humanity. The teachings of Jesus, which transcended mere philosophy, could engage with these ideas, fulfilling the deep longings of the human soul.

"Language of the Gospel"

From Greece's rise, a language spread,
Uniting worlds where thoughts were led.
In cities, temples, homes, and halls,
The gospel echoed through their walls.

From east to west, a language shared,
A tool for truth, for those who cared.
The Greeks allowed the gospel call,
That Christ's story might reach all

- Hellenization: Greek influence spread the language and culture of Greece throughout the Mediterranean world. The widespread use of Greek made it easier for the message of Jesus and the early church writings to be understood in diverse regions. The apostle Paul's letters and the New Testament were written in Greek, allowing them to be shared widely in the world of that time.

- Philosophical Environment: Greek philosophers had explored deep questions about God, ethics, and humanity. The teachings of Jesus and the apostles could engage with these ideas, showing how the gospel was the fulfillment of many philosophical and religious questions. As Acts 17:28 affirms, *"In Him we live and move and have our being,"* illustrating how Greek thought paved the way for the gospel to connect with the spiritual needs of the people.

Segment 4: The Roman Empire's Contribution

The Roman Empire (63 B.C. - A.D. 1453) brought about a significant political environment that made the spread of the gospel possible. The Romans created the Pax Romana—a period of relative peace and stability across the empire. This peace allowed for safer travel and communication, which was vital for the apostles as they traveled to spread the message of Jesus.

In addition, the Romans built an extensive system of roads that connected cities and regions, making travel easier and more efficient. These roads, along with Roman laws and governance, helped create a sense of unity and order, providing the infrastructure needed for the gospel to spread far and wide.

"Roads and Peace"

Upon the Roman roads they trod,

The apostles preached the Word of God.

Through roads and peace, the world was tied,

A path for truth, both far and wide.

Though emperors ruled with iron hand,

God's kingdom spread across the land.

The Pax Romana, safe and free,

Opened the world for all to see.

- *Pax Romana*: The peace established by the Roman Empire provided a stable environment in which the message of Jesus could spread. Without this peace, the risks and dangers of travel would have hindered missionary work. The Apostle Paul, for example, benefited from this stability when traveling throughout the Roman world.
- Roman Roads: The extensive network of Roman roads allowed missionaries, including Paul, to travel quickly and safely throughout the empire, spreading the gospel across large distances. As Acts 13:4-5 illustrates, the apostles relied on the roads to carry their message far and wide.
- Roman Law: Roman legal systems allowed for the protection of early Christians, as Paul often appealed to Roman law to safeguard his ministry. This legal protection also allowed the apostles to spread their message with less fear of persecution, facilitating the rapid expansion of Christianity.

Conclusion: The Fullness of Time

When Jesus came into the world, the fullness of time had arrived. God had sovereignly orchestrated the rise and fall of nations to prepare the world for the arrival of the Messiah. Each empire contributed in unique ways: the Persian Empire laid the foundation for the restoration of the Jewish people; the Greek Empire spread a common language that unified vast regions; and the Roman Empire provided peace, roads, and legal structures that enabled the spread of the gospel. This convergence of empires was no accident, but a manifestation of God's sovereign plan to bring His Kingdom to earth.

"A Time of God's Design"

In the fullness of time, God's plan unfolds,
The nations prepared, the story's told.
Persia to Greece, to Rome, to all lands,
God's Kingdom comes by mighty hand.
The world was set, the path made clear,
The Savior came, drawing us near.
In the fullness of time, He made His way,
To redeem the world on that holy day.

God's Master Plan

The convergence of these empires and their contributions created an environment in which the gospel could spread quickly and effectively. This was not a coincidence but the result of God's sovereign orchestration. As Daniel 2:21 declares, God *"removes kings and sets up kings,"* directing history toward His divine purposes.

Paul speaks of the perfect timing of Jesus' arrival—*the fullness of time* (Gal. 4:4-5). This was the optimal moment for the gospel to spread through the world. All preceding events and empires laid the foundation for this pivotal moment in history orchestrated by God.

Reflections

1. How does seeing God's hand in the rise and fall of empires—Persia, Greece, Rome—change the way we view current world events and our role within them as Kingdom people?
2. In what ways do you think God may be using the systems, languages, or technologies of our time to prepare for future Kingdom work, just as He used roads, law, and language in the ancient world?

5

The Kingdom of the Stone

In the dream of Nebuchadnezzar, king of Babylon, a vision unfolded that reached far beyond his empire (Dan. 2). Daniel interpreted the statue the king saw: a head of gold—Babylon; chest and arms of silver—Medo-Persia; belly and thighs of bronze—Greece; legs of iron and feet mixed with clay—Rome. All these kingdoms would fall. Then came a stone, not cut by human hands, that struck the statue and shattered it. The stone grew into a mountain filling the world.

This stone, Daniel revealed, represented God's Kingdom—unlike any the world had known. Not built by human strength, nor dependent on military power or political strategy, it would rise, triumph, and never end. It would begin small, almost imperceptibly, but surpass all earthly empires in scope and permanence.

Centuries later, the Kingdom began to take form—not as a political movement, but in the life, death, and resurrection of Jesus. He was the stone rejected by the builders, the cornerstone of God's new creation (1 Peter 2:6-8). In Jesus, the Kingdom became both a present reality and a future hope.

Jesus spoke of His Kingdom not in terms of earthly power but spiritual renewal. *"My kingdom is not of this world"* (John 18:36). His reign begins in the hearts of those who follow Him. It's not about force or territory, but about transformation and submission to God's will. This Kingdom brings redemption, peace, and unity, not conquest.

Jesus proclaimed that the Kingdom had already come—and yet it was still coming. Like the stone in the dream, it would grow to fill the earth, transcending borders and cultures, never to be overthrown.

"The Kingdom of the Stone"

The dream of a king, in his bed he lay,
Of kingdoms that rise, kingdoms that sway.
A statue of gold, of silver, and brass,
The might of the earth, like seasons, would pass.

But then, from the sky, a stone did fall,
Not made by the hands, no craftsmen at all.
It struck the feet, the statue did break,
Its rise declared, the world at stake.

A kingdom that grew, filled all the land,
Not forged by hands, nor by man's command.
A mountain that rose from the smallest of stones,
It filled the earth, and it claimed its throne.

Kingdom of God, not bound by years,
Not built by hands, by blood, nor by fears.
It crushes kingdoms, and stands in light,
Kingdom eternal, with God its might.

A stone that was cast, a Kingdom that grew,
Its walls salvation, its gates are truth.
A Kingdom eternal, forever will stand,
The rule of the King in every land.

A New Kind of Kingdom

The Kingdom of God, represented by the stone, is profoundly different from earthly power. In Jesus' time, many expected a political Messiah who would overthrow Roman rule. But Jesus brought something far greater: the reign of God in the hearts of people. This Kingdom wasn't about territory or armies. It was spiritual and deeply personal. Like a seed, it starts small but grows into something vast. Jesus used the parable of the mustard seed (Matt. 13:31–32) to show that what begins tiny can transform the world.

The stone shatters the empires of the world, not with force but by divine authority. Earthly kingdoms rise and fall. God's Kingdom is eternal, unshakable, built on the foundation of Jesus—the rejected stone who became the cornerstone.

Jesus' ministry marked the arrival of this Kingdom. His miracles, teachings, and death revealed God's reign on earth. Yet He taught us to pray, *"Your Kingdom come,"* pointing to a fullness still ahead.

The Kingdom keeps expanding. It cannot be confined to one nation or time. It spans the globe and reaches into every culture. The church is its visible expression—living, proclaiming, and embodying the Kingdom today.

Key Aspects of the Kingdom of God:

- **Spiritual in Nature**: Not of this world; built through Christ's life, death, and resurrection.
- **Marked by Peace and Justice**: Unlike human kingdoms built through war and pride, this Kingdom brings reconciliation.
- **Steadily Growing**: Like a stone becoming a mountain, as in Nebuchadnezzar's dream, it expands through the gospel.
- **Transformative**: It changes hearts and lives, even now, through the Spirit's power.
- **Eternal**: It will endure forever, fully realized when Christ returns and all is made new.

Conclusion

The Kingdom of the Stone is not a kingdom that operates by the principles of the world. It is a kingdom that begins small, in the heart of one person at a time, and slowly spreads across the world. It will ultimately fill the entire earth, transcending borders, nations, and peoples. This Kingdom is one of peace, justice, and transformation, and it will endure forever. Jesus is its King, and His reign is one of love, grace, and redemption. As we await the full manifestation of God's Kingdom, we are called to live as citizens of that eternal Kingdom, faithfully engaging with the kingdoms of this world.

Reflections

1. What does the image of the stone becoming a mountain reveal about how God's Kingdom operates compared to earthly kingdoms? How does this image challenge the way we typically think about power, growth, and influence?

2. Jesus said, *"My kingdom is not of this world"* (John 18:36). In what ways does this truth shape how we engage with politics, culture, and power structures in our own day?

3. The Kingdom begins in the heart, but grows to fill the world. How does this progression encourage both personal transformation and global mission?

4. Earthly kingdoms rise and fall, but God's Kingdom endures. What does this truth offer us in times of global uncertainty, conflict, or cultural decline?

Notes for your Journal:

6

Speaking Forth God's Word

The Old Testament is filled with prophecies pointing to a coming Messiah, a figure who would deliver Israel from oppression, restore justice, and establish God's Kingdom on earth. For centuries, these prophecies fueled the Jewish people's anticipation, especially during the time of Roman occupation, when they longed for a political and military leader to restore their nation.

The prophets were not fore-tellers, not predictors of the future. They were "forth tellers." Inspired by God, they spoke forth His word. Often, they communicated a message that they themselves could not fully understand. Recall for example, Isaiah called Cyrus, a king yet to come, by name—176 years before he led his armies to overthrow Babylon and free the Jews from captivity.

The prophets were not looking into crystal balls or reading tea leaves. They were simply listening to God and declaring, "*Thus saith the Lord.*" They weren't seeing the future—God was. And the future was one that God was guiding toward a singular, divine point: the coming of His Son, the *Logos*, incarnate.

The prophets proclaimed that a Savior was coming. Yet, Jesus' fulfillment of these prophecies took many by surprise. While deeply rooted in God's promises, His mission was not what the people expected. They anticipated a political conqueror, a leader to restore the nation of Israel and overthrow their Roman oppressors. Instead, Jesus came as a spiritual Savior, whose work of redemption would transcend national and political boundaries, offering salvation to the whole world.

We will explore four key prophecies. (The Bible contains many more. These are chosen merely as representative of that larger body of messages from our transcendent God.) Each of these shaped the Jewish understanding of the Messiah and shed light on the nature of Jesus' mission.

These prophecies would not be fulfilled through earthly political upheaval, but through divine intervention—culminating in Jesus' birth, life, death, and resurrection. His fulfillment of these promises would redefine the very concept of the Messiah, offering a salvation that was not bound by human expectations, but grounded in God's eternal purpose.

The Virgin Birth

Prophecy: Isaiah 7:14 states: *"Therefore the Lord himself will give you a sign. Behold, the virgin shall conceive and bear a son, and shall call his name Immanuel."*

The prophecy of the virgin birth was originally a sign given to King Ahaz during a time of national crisis. It was intended to reassure him of God's presence in the midst of looming political threats. However, Christian tradition sees this prophecy as pointing to the miraculous birth of Jesus. The term "Immanuel" (*"God with us"*) reveals the nature of the Messiah as both fully human and fully divine. Jesus' birth, in humble circumstances to a virgin named Mary, signifies God's intervention in history to redeem humanity.

This event marked the beginning of God's Kingdom breaking into the world, not through political force but through the humble, loving presence of God among His people.

"The Sign of Immanuel"

A child, a gift, a holy sign,
A virgin's womb, the Lord divine
In Bethlehem, on quiet night,
A star proclaimed the coming light.

Immanuel, God with us here,
In human form, drawing near.
The promise given long ago,
Now in this child, the world would know.
Not throne of gold nor crown with pride,
But in a manger, He would abide.
A King, a Savior, born to be,
The hope of all eternity.
So let the heavens sing His praise,
For in His birth, we find our grace.
Immanuel, the promised One,
God's redemption has begun.

Analysis: Isaiah 7:14 touches on a foundational theological theme: the incarnation. God does not remain distant but becomes fully present among His people. The virgin birth challenges worldly expectations of power and kingship, signaling that God's method of redemption would be unlike any other. The prophecy foreshadows the dual nature of Jesus as both human and divine, laying the groundwork for understanding His role in salvation history. This theme of God with us (Immanuel) ties directly into the New Testament revelation that Jesus' life, death, and resurrection embody the fulfillment of God's promise of presence, guidance, and deliverance.

The Birthplace of the Messiah

Prophecy: Micah 5:2 states: *"But you, O Bethlehem Ephrathah, who are too little to be among the clans of Judah, from you shall come forth for me one who is to be ruler in Israel, whose coming forth is from of old, from ancient days."*

Micah's prophecy highlights the seemingly insignificant town of Bethlehem as the birthplace of Israel's ruler. Though small and unremarkable, Bethlehem had the profound honor of being the birthplace of King David, and by extension, it would become the birthplace of the Messiah. Jesus' birth in Bethlehem fulfilled the ancient promise that the Messiah would come from the line of David, despite the town's lowly status. The humble nature of His birth in this tiny village would challenge preconceived notions about the Messiah's identity and reign.

"Bethlehem's Promise"

O little town, so small, so still,
Where ancient prophets' words fulfill.
In humble streets, a King is born,
To lead the world, the light of dawn.
Bethlehem, you hold the key,
To God's own plan of history.
From David's line, the ruler's rise,
A King who wears no earthly guise.
No royal throne, no palace grand,
Just heaven's promise, in this land.
A child to change the world, indeed,
The Savior born to meet our need.
O Bethlehem, you held the light,
That pierced the world's darkest night.
And in that manger, small and bare,
The hope of all was born right there.

Analysis: The prophecy of Micah 5:2 reinforces the theme of God's sovereignty in choosing unexpected vessels to fulfill His redemptive plan. Jesus' birth in Bethlehem emphasizes God's choice of the humble and small over the powerful and grand. This establishes a consistent biblical theme: God does not choose the ways of the world but instead works through humility and weakness to accomplish His mighty purposes. Jesus' birthplace further signals that God's kingdom is not of this world, laying the foundation for the spiritual nature of His rule.

The Humble King

Prophecy: Zechariah 9:9 states: *"Rejoice greatly, O daughter of Zion! Shout aloud, O daughter of Jerusalem! Behold, your king is coming to you; righteous and having salvation is he, humble and mounted on a donkey, on a colt, the foal of a donkey."*

Zechariah's prophecy depicts a King who arrives in peace, not war. By choosing to ride on a donkey instead of a horse, Jesus fulfills this prophecy in a manner that confounds the expectations of the people. The crowds expected a political liberator who would free them from Roman rule, but Jesus came to establish peace, not through military might, but through His death and resurrection. His triumphal entry into Jerusalem, although celebrated, was a stark contrast to the political and military uprisings they hoped for.

"The Humble King"

Rejoice, O Zion, sing and shout,
Your King is here, let none doubt.
Not on a stallion, proud and tall,
But on a donkey, He comes to call.
Righteous and humble, He rides in peace,
The King of Glory, brings release.
Not to conquer with sword or spear,
But to bring salvation, cast out fear.
Hosanna! The crowd cries in delight,
Not knowing the cost of this royal sight.
The King, crowned with thorns, would reign,
And through His death, all lives would gain.
Oh, humble King, whose reign has come,
A Kingdom of peace, of hearts undone.
In quiet strength, You take Your throne,
A Savior who calls all, "Come home."

Analysis: Zechariah 9:9 encapsulates the theme of the "already but not yet" kingdom of God. Jesus' peaceful arrival on a donkey contrasts sharply with expectations of a warrior king. This points to the nature of His first coming: to bring salvation through humility and suffering. His kingship is established not through violent overthrow, but through sacrificial love, setting the foundation for the Christian understanding of the Kingdom of God.

His reign is not of this world, and this reshapes our understanding of power, kingship, and salvation. Jesus, as the humble King, introduces a new kind of victory—one that is achieved through the cross rather than the sword.

Conclusion

By expanding on each of the prophecies, we see how they not only fulfill specific expectations but also unfold a greater theological narrative: the coming of the Messiah redefines power, salvation, and kingship. Through His humble birth, birthplace, and entry into Jerusalem, Jesus inaugurates a kingdom built on peace, justice, and love rather than military might. These prophecies provide deep insight into the nature of the Messiah and invite us into a broader understanding of God's redemptive plan.

Reflections

1. Why is it important to understand the prophets as "forth-tellers" rather than mere predictors of the future?

2. Each prophecy highlighted reveals something unexpected about the Messiah. Which one challenged your assumptions the most—and why?

3. How does Jesus' fulfillment of these Old Testament prophecies reshape the way we think about strength, leadership, and victory in God's Kingdom?

4. What does the contrast between worldly power and divine humility teach us about the ways God works in history—and in our lives?

7

The Suffering Servant

The Jewish people were awaiting a Messiah—a Savior who would deliver them from oppression and reestablish the Kingdom of Israel. Their expectations, shaped by centuries of prophetic writings, imagined a Messiah who would be a mighty king, a political leader who would overthrow Israel's enemies. However, as they came to realize, the fulfillment of the prophecies was not what they had imagined. The most shocking element was not just how Jesus came, but what He would endure—the sufferings He would face to fulfill God's plan for redemption.

Isaiah's prophecy about the "Suffering Servant" is one of the most profound and paradoxical of all the Messianic prophecies. Rather than a triumphant political figure, Isaiah speaks of a servant who would suffer, be rejected, and be wounded for the sake of others. These prophecies, particularly found in Isaiah 52:13-53:12, paint a picture of a servant who, though despised and forsaken, would bring healing and salvation through His suffering.

These passages would have been difficult for many to comprehend, as they conflicted with the more common expectations of a conquering king. Yet, for Christians, these prophecies were not just about a suffering figure; they were about Jesus—the one who came to redeem humanity by taking upon Himself the sins of the world.

As Jesus moved toward the cross, He embodied these prophecies, showing that the true nature of His kingship was one of self-sacrificial love. The Suffering Servant would not rule through might, but through laying down His life for others. In His suffering, He would accomplish the very purpose for which He was sent: to save, heal, and redeem all who would believe in Him.

The connection between the Suffering Servant of Isaiah and Jesus' life and death is unmistakable (see Acts 8:29-35). This is where the true nature of the Kingdom of God is revealed—not in worldly power, but in the power of love and sacrifice.

"The Suffering Servant"
Behold the Servant, despised and low,
King with no crown, heart full of woe.
He carries our griefs, He bears our shame,
Rejected, forsaken, still called by name.
Wounded for us, He takes our place,
With every stripe, He offers grace.
Led as a lamb, silent and meek,
For healing all, the lost, the weak.
Upon the cross, His life is poured,
The Lamb of God, our Savior, Lord.
He knew no sin, yet He bore it all,
To lift us up, to answer the call.
Through suffering, redemption flows,
In His pain, our salvation grows.
This humble King, in whose reign is love,
Brings peace on earth, hope from above.
O Suffering Servant, our hearts receive,
Your mercy and grace, we do believe.
For through Your wounds, we are made whole,
You heal our hearts, You save our souls.

The Suffering Servant and the Nature of the Kingdom
The Suffering Servant prophecies in Isaiah are some of the most profound and revealing passages in all of Scripture. They depict a figure who was not expected by the people of Israel—a figure who would not come in glory and power, but in humility and suffering. These prophecies challenge the expectations of a Messiah who

would restore Israel through military victory. Instead, Isaiah presents a Servant who would bring healing to the world not through military might, but through His own suffering and sacrifice.

- **Suffering and Redemption**: Isaiah 53 describes the Servant as *"despised and rejected by men,"* a man of sorrows who *"bore our griefs"* and *"carried our sorrows."* These words seem incomprehensible in light of the traditional expectation of a conquering Messiah. Yet, it is through this suffering that the Servant would accomplish the work of redemption. Jesus' death on the cross would fulfill this prophecy in the most complete and profound way. He would suffer in our place, bearing the punishment for sin that we deserve, and in doing so, He would bring us healing—spiritual restoration and peace with God.

- **A Different Kind of King**: The Suffering Servant is not a political ruler; He is a servant, one who lays down His life for others. This foreshadows the radical nature of Jesus' kingship. Jesus' rule is not established through force, but through sacrificial love. His kingship is defined by humility, grace, and a willingness to endure suffering for the sake of His people. This is the heart of the Kingdom of God: built not on military conquest, but on selfless service; giving of one's life for others.

- **The Fulfillment in Jesus**: For Christians, the Suffering Servant prophecies point directly to Jesus. His life, death, and resurrection are the fulfillment of Isaiah's words. Jesus' suffering on the cross was not an unfortunate accident; it was the very purpose for which He came into the world. Through His suffering, He would bring redemption to humanity. The cross is not just a symbol of death; it is the symbol of life—life offered freely for the salvation of the world.

- **The Kingdom of Peace and Justice**: Jesus, the Suffering Servant, also represents the true nature of the Kingdom of God.

The Kingdom He came to establish is not one of violence and oppression, but one of peace, justice, and reconciliation. The Kingdom of God is characterized by love and sacrifice. In Jesus' life and death, He demonstrated what it means to seek first the Kingdom—not through power, but through love and sacrifice.

- **A Call to Follow**: The Suffering Servant also calls His followers to a different kind of life. Jesus' life challenges His disciples to follow in His footsteps, to take up their crosses, and to serve others humbly. The path of the Kingdom is one of self-giving love, not one of selfish ambition. Jesus invites all who follow Him to embrace the cost of discipleship, which is not worldly power, but the power of love and service.

In light of these reflections, it is clear that the Suffering Servant prophecies of Isaiah offer us a deeper understanding of Jesus' mission and the nature of the Kingdom He came to establish. Far from being a Messiah of military conquest, Jesus came as the Servant King, bringing salvation through His suffering. His death on the cross was not the end of His story, but the beginning of the fulfillment of God's plan to restore humanity to Himself.

These prophecies shape our understanding of what it means to live in the Kingdom of God. We are called to embrace the way of the Servant, following Jesus' example of humility, sacrifice, and love. The Suffering Servant reveals the true power of God's Kingdom: to heal, to restore, and to bring peace through the selfless love.

Reflections

1. How does the image of a suffering, rejected Savior challenge our assumptions about what strength and leadership look like—in faith, in life, or in society?
2. In what ways are we personally called to reflect the heart of the Suffering Servant in how we live, lead, and love others today?

8

Angels: Messengers of God
—Attendants to the King

Angels, often viewed through a lens shaped by popular culture, are far more than the whimsical beings depicted in cartoons and artwork. The Bible presents them as powerful, divine agents of God's will—unseen warriors of light, delivering His messages and executing His purposes in the world. As Billy Graham famously described them, angels are "God's secret agents," and their role is not only to guide and protect but also to proclaim, warn, and declare the eternal truths of the kingdom of God.

Angels are not weak, mythological creatures, nor are they merely ethereal beings strumming harps on clouds. Rather, they are fierce, celestial warriors unmatched by any force known to humanity. The Bible speaks of their power—describing tens of thousands of angels surrounding God when He gave Moses the Law (Deut. 33:2) and even revealing that Jesus could have called upon 12 legions of angels—60,000 angelic warriors—at His command (Matt. 26:53).

These divine messengers are present not only in times of spiritual need but also in pivotal moments of history. Their very existence and actions remind us that the spiritual realm is far more powerful than anything in the physical world. In the Old Testament, Elisha's servant was initially terrified when he saw the Syrian army surrounding them. But when his eyes were opened, he saw that the hills were filled with angels—an army of fire, stronger than anything visible (2 Kings 6:16-17).

In the Garden of Gethsemane, when Jesus was about to be arrested, He could have summoned angelic armies at a moment's no-tice, yet He chose not to. This silent strength, unseen and untouched by earthly forces, speaks volumes about their power and purpose. They do not draw attention to themselves, but rather point to the glory of God.

The presence of angels brings to life the profound truth that God's purposes are unfolding in powerful, often unseen ways—reminding us that the unseen forces of heaven are always at work in the world. And so, when angels appear in the narrative of Jesus' life, they do not simply deliver a message; they fulfill the most significant roles in the story of redemption.

"Messengers of God"
"Chosen to Proclaim Good News"
Before the fullness of time had come,
God sent His messengers, one by one.
The angel Gabriel, chosen to declare,
The birth of a Child beyond compare.
To Mary, a virgin, in Nazareth's street,
The angel spoke of a Savior's deed.
"Rejoice, O favored one, for you will bear,
The Son of God—His love and care."
The heavens, too, would soon declare,
The birth of the Savior, beyond compare.
In the silence of night, the angels sing,
"Glory to God, the newborn King!"

"Birth: Angels at the Stable"
In the darkness of Bethlehem's night,
A Child was born, a beacon of light.
The angels stood above the land,
Proclaiming love with voice so grand.
To shepherds, they came, shining bright,
Bringing good news, breaking the night.

"Fear not," they said, "we bring you cheer,
A Savior is born—bring Him near!"
A host of angels joined in praise,
Proclaiming peace in endless ways.
For in that moment, God came near,
To offer love, His grace sincere.

"The Wilderness: Temptation and Protection"
In the wilderness, desert dry,
Jesus faced the tempter, with just reply.
But as He stood, firm in His trust,
He believed God's word—faithful and just.
Satan's words were harsh and cold,
Angels came their Prince to uphold.
They came to strengthen, comfort, cheer.
The Son of God would persevere.
In this dark moment of trial and pain,
The angel's presence was Jesus' gain.
As they ministered to Him without fuss,
Ministering spirits are they to us.

"Resurrection: The Glory of the Lord"
When the stone was rolled away,
And dawn broke the silence of that day,
Two angels appeared, dressed in light,
Announcing victory, pure and bright.
"Why seek you the living among the dead?"
They spoke, with glory in what they said.
"He is risen, as He said—go, proclaim!
The Savior has conquered death and shame."
The messengers of glory, shining bright,
Declared that death no longer held might.
In that moment, the angels rejoiced,
For God's redemption had been voiced.

"Ascension: Returning to the Heavens"
As Jesus rose beyond their sight,
The angels asked with voices bright:
"Why stand you here gazing so?
He'll come again as you saw Him go."
They came to still the grieving crowd—
Though sorrow lingered like a shroud—
He shall return in pow'r and light,
As King of kings to set things right.
God's messengers, still bearing grace,
Speak truth for every time and place.
From manger low to empty tomb,
Their witness shines through joy and gloom.

Analysis: The Role of Angels in the Christ Event

Angels are not merely celestial beings; they are essential messengers through whom God reveals His plan of salvation. Their presence underscores the profound connection between the heavenly realm and earthly realities. The role they play in the Christ event is both protective and declarative, as they announce, affirm, and strengthen God's will and plan.

- **Pre-Birth:** The angel Gabriel's visit to Mary marked the first announcement of the Messiah's coming, breaking a silence that had lasted for centuries. Gabriel's message was a declaration of divine intervention, telling Mary she would bear the Son of God, defying natural law. The angels' messages were not merely declarations—they were invitations to enter into the unfolding divine mystery—a virgin conception.

- **Birth:** At Jesus' birth, angels heralded His arrival with heavenly praise. Their song was not just one of worship, but a proclamation that the Kingdom of God had arrived in the form of a child. The angels made clear that, while His birth was humble in setting, it was momentous in the cosmic story of redemption.

- **Wilderness:** In the wilderness, Jesus was tempted by Satan to determine what kind of Messiah He would be. After days of fasting, prayer, and meditation, Satan tested Him. Remaining true to the Father's intent, Jesus rebuffed every test. When Satan departed, angels came and ministered to Him. This moment reveals the intimate relationship between the divine and the human, even in the harshest trials.

- **Resurrection:** At the resurrection, angels bore the good news. They reminded the women at the tomb that Jesus had risen just as He had promised. Their role is to point people to the truth of God's promises and to reveal the glory of God's ultimate victory over death.

- **Ascension:** Finally, at the ascension, angels served as messengers of hope, reminding the disciples that Jesus would return. Their words reassured the followers of Christ that His mission was far from over and that His return would be in power and glory. The angels' reminder carries eschatological weight: the story of redemption is still unfolding, and the final chapter is yet to come.

Throughout the entire narrative, angels act as God's heralds, constantly reminding humanity of His sovereign plan and the significance of the Christ event. Their words and actions provide clarity and direction, ensuring that the message of Christ's birth, death, and resurrection would reach the world. In each instance, the angels do more than deliver news—they invite humanity to participate in the divine story of salvation.

Their role reinforces the theme that God's will, which transcends time and space, is always at work, even through unexpected messengers. The angels of the Christ event remind us that God's purposes unfold in the most profound and mysterious ways, inviting us to listen, respond, and join in the eternal chorus of praise to the God who has come to redeem the world.

Reflections

1. Angels served at key moments in Jesus' life—not to draw attention to themselves, but to point to God's purposes. How might this shape our own understanding of faithful service, the message we are to proclaim, and spiritual humility?

2. From Gabriel's announcement to the message at the empty tomb, angels were bearers of divine truth. In what ways can we become faithful messengers of God's hope in our own time and place?

3. The angels reminded the disciples at the ascension that Christ would return. How does this forward-looking hope shape how we live in the present?

4. The invisible presence of angels reminds us of the unseen spiritual reality behind what we can see. How does this truth challenge or encourage your understanding of God's nearness in everyday life?

Notes for your Journal:

9

The Annunciation
(Luke 1:26–38)

The Annunciation marks the moment when the angel Gabriel appears to Mary in Nazareth, delivering the incredible news that she will conceive a child by the Holy Spirit—God's Son, the long-awaited Messiah. Mary, a young woman betrothed to Joseph, is perplexed and initially troubled by the angel's greeting and message. The angel reassures her, explaining that this child will be *"great"* and will *"reign over the house of Jacob forever,"* fulfilling the promise made to King David.

This announcement is not just about the birth of a child but the fulfillment of prophecy. It speaks of God's active intervention in the world, bringing salvation through His Son, who will rule an eternal kingdom. The moment is rich with theological and messianic implications, placing Mary at the center of God's redemptive plan.

But this call came with risk. In Mary's world, pregnancy outside of marriage could lead to public shame, exclusion, or even death by stoning under the law. Her betrothal to Joseph would be threatened, her reputation shattered, and her future uncertain. She had no experience to guide her, no assurance of how Joseph—or her community—would respond. Yet she answered, *"I am the Lord's servant. May your word to me be fulfilled."* Her obedience reveals the courageous faith of a young woman who trusted God's plan more than she feared the consequences.

Mary becomes not only the mother of Jesus, but a model of discipleship. She shows us what it means to surrender completely to the call of God, even when it defies logic, tradition, and personal safety.

"The Annunciation"

In the quiet town of Nazareth,
A young heart beat in simple faith,
Unknowing that the world would turn,
With a single word, her life would shake.
The angel's voice, a call so clear,
"Rejoice, O Mary, favored dear!
You will conceive, by Spirit's grace,
The Holy One will fill your space."
She asked the angel, "How can this be?
A mystery beyond what eyes could see.
"Do not fear," the angel said,
"God's hand upon you is gently laid."
A promise made, a King to come,
The throne of David, His kingdom won.
Through you, the world will know His name,
His reign eternal—none shall claim.
She trembled, yet with faith she bowed,
Her heart was pure, her soul unbowed.
"I am the servant of the Lord,
Let it be done, by Your Word."
And so it was—God's will proclaimed,
A virgin's heart in faith unchained.
The Savior's call, the world's reply,
In Mary's trust, God's plan took flight.

Analysis:

- **Messianic Fulfillment:** This scene directly addresses messianic expectations. Gabriel's message to Mary speaks of the fulfillment of God's promises to David and to Israel. The Messiah, who was expected to come as a deliverer, a king in the line of David, is revealed as a humble child. Yet, this child will be *"great"* and will *"reign forever,"* embodying the eternal kingdom that the Jews had longed for. The initial shock and confusion Mary feels are understandable—she was expecting a kingdom of power and military might, but God's kingdom would come through humility and divine intervention.

- **The Role of Mary:** Mary's response encapsulates the heart of obedience and submission to God's will. Her "Yes" is a key turning point in God's redemptive plan. By accepting her role, she becomes a model of faith for all believers. Her acceptance of God's calling, even though it was an unimaginable and risky proposition, highlights the nature of true discipleship.

- **Theological Implications:** Theologically, this passage introduces the concept of the Incarnation—God becoming man in the person of Jesus Christ. This divine mystery is captured in the angel's words: *"The Holy Spirit will come on you, and the power of the Most High will overshadow you."* The idea that the eternal God would take on human flesh in such an intimate and vulnerable way through Mary speaks to the depth of God's love and commitment to His creation.

- **Connection to the Old Testament:** Gabriel's words to Mary echo the promises made to King David, showing that Jesus is the fulfillment of God's covenant with Israel. This is a powerful link between the Old and New Testaments, demonstrating that Jesus is the Messiah they had long awaited, though His arrival is unexpected in its form.

Reflections

1. **Mary's "yes" to God came at great personal risk.** What might this reveal about the nature of true obedience and faith in the face of cultural pressure or uncertainty?

2. **The angel's message to Mary was both terrifying and wondrous.** How do you think fear and faith can coexist in moments

when God calls us into something unexpected?

3. **Mary likely had very little understanding of how this would unfold.** What does her response teach us about saying "yes" to God when we don't have all the answers?

4. **The Incarnation began with a quiet moment and a willing heart.** How might we make ourselves more available to the surprising ways God might want to use us?

Notes for your Journal:

10

The Magnificat

(Luke 1:46-55)

The Magnificat is Mary's song of praise to God after her visit to
her cousin Elizabeth, who is also miraculously pregnant with
John the Baptist. Mary's proclamation is filled with joy, recognizing God's great favor upon her, but also acknowledging His justice and mercy. In the Magnificat, Mary sings of God's reversal
of earthly values—lifting up the lowly and bringing down the
powerful, filling the hungry with good things and sending the rich
away empty. She celebrates God's faithfulness to His promises,
acknowledging that He has helped His servant Israel and will
continue to remember His covenant with Abraham.

Mary's journey to see Elizabeth was not just a family visit—
it was a refuge. In the aftermath of Gabriel's announcement,
Mary was carrying a secret no one would easily believe. Her visit
to Elizabeth, who was experiencing her own miracle in old age,
created a sacred space of mutual understanding. Elizabeth's greeting confirmed the angel's words and offered a balm to Mary's
uncertainty: *"Blessed are you among women, and blessed is the
fruit of your womb"* (Luke 1:42). In that moment, Mary's burden
became praise.

Elizabeth's pregnancy with John the Baptist—long thought
impossible—served as a sign of God's faithfulness, both to her
and to Mary. Together, these women stood as living testimonies
to God's power: one bearing the forerunner, the other the Messiah. Their embrace was not just familial; it was prophetic—a

meeting of grace and purpose, woven into the unfolding drama of redemption.

It is in this environment—safe, Spirit-filled, and affirming—that Mary finds her voice and lifts it in song. Her Magnificat flows not from certainty of what the future will hold, but from assurance in the One who holds the future. In Elizabeth's presence, Mary realizes she is not alone—and through that realization, she proclaims the faithfulness of a God who lifts the lowly and remembers His promises.

The Magnificat is a powerful declaration of the themes that will run throughout Jesus' life: God's kingdom is one of humility, justice, and mercy. Mary's words echo the messianic prophecies of the Old Testament, which anticipated the coming of a Savior who would bring justice, peace, and restoration. Her song captures the essence of God's redemptive work and serves as a proclamation of the arrival of the Messiah, whose reign would bring about the ultimate fulfillment of all God's promises.

"The Magnificat"

My soul magnifies the Lord on high,
With joy, my spirit lifts to the sky.
For He has looked on me with favor,
A humble servant—His love to savor.

From this day forth, all will call me blessed,
The Mighty One has done what's best.
Holy is His name, forever pure,
His mercy, for those who endure.

His arm has struck with power and might,
Casting down the proud from their height.
The lowly He lifts, the meek He exalts,
In His kingdom, no one falters.

He fills the hungry, their needs He meets,
And sends the rich away in defeat.
He's come to save, to heal, to mend,
To make things right, to bring the end.

Israel's God, faithful and true,
Has remembered the promises He knew.
To Abraham's seed, He's made a way,
A Savior borne, this blessed day.

My soul magnifies the Lord on high,
His mercy, endless as the sky.
I praise Him now and evermore,
For He has come to heal and restore.

Analysis:

- **Messianic Implications:** The Magnificat emphasizes the messianic reversal that Jesus' arrival brings. Mary's song celebrates God's faithfulness to His promises, and it speaks to the central mission of the Messiah—lifting the lowly and humbling the proud. This would come to full fruition in Jesus' ministry, as He brought a message of hope and justice for the poor, the oppressed, and the marginalized.

- **Reversal of Expectations:** One of the key themes in the Magnificat is the reversal of worldly expectations. Where society values power, wealth, and status, God's kingdom values humility, mercy, and justice. This theme runs through the Gospel of Luke and is evident in Jesus' teachings and actions. Mary's song is prophetic, declaring that God's justice will come to those who have been oppressed, and that the powerful will be brought low.

- **Theological Depth:** The Magnificat reveals deep theological truths about God's nature and His redemptive plan. It emphasizes His mercy, justice, and faithfulness, and it serves as a powerful expression of the coming kingdom that Jesus would inaugurate. It's a song of liberation, of hope for the downtrodden, and of faith in God's unfailing promises.

These two key moments from Luke's Gospel—**The Annunciation** and **The Magnificat**—are foundational for understanding Jesus' messianic mission. They lay the groundwork for the themes that unfolded in His ministry and provided deep insights into the nature of the kingdom He came to establish.

Reflections

1. Mary's Magnificat is a song of praise born from both faith and struggle. How can moments of uncertainty become fertile ground for deeper worship and trust?

2. Elizabeth created a safe space for Mary to be seen and believed. Who in your life has offered you spiritual encouragement in a time of risk or vulnerability? How can you be that person for someone else?

3. The Magnificat declares a God who brings down the proud and lifts up the humble. What does this say about the values of God's kingdom versus those of our culture?

4. Mary's song affirms God's faithfulness to His promises. In what ways can remembering God's past faithfulness strengthen our hope for what He has yet to do?

11

The Mystery of the Incarnate *Logos*
—Self-Limitation

In Philippians 2:5-11, the Apostle Paul paints a profound picture of the *Logos*—the Word of God, who is fully divine, yet voluntarily took on the form of a servant. The passage stands as a theological masterpiece, addressing the union of divinity and humanity in the person of Jesus Christ. Central to this passage is the idea of *kenosis*—the self-emptying of the *Logos*, but not in the sense of losing His divine essence. Rather, He voluntarily laid aside the privileges and prerogatives that came with His divine glory, choosing to live among us as fully human.

This concept, rooted deeply in Scripture, challenges many traditional understandings of the human being named Jesus. To the devout, He is often seen as "God among us," and yet the Bible presents a more subtle and powerful mystery. Jesus, the incarnated *Logos*, refrained from the full exercise of His divine powers, choosing instead to embrace the human condition—vulnerable, dependent, and fully surrendered to the Father's will.

1. Kenosis: Not the Loss of Divinity, But Laying Aside Glory
Theologians have long debated the meaning of *kenosis*, with divergent views often influenced by tradition. Some have suggested that the *Logos* emptied Himself of His divinity in the incarnation. But as Joseph Henry Thayer wisely points out, the term *ekenosen* (from the Greek verb *kenóo*) suggests not a loss but a voluntary laying aside. Jesus did not cease to be divine when He became incarnate; rather, He chose to function within the limitations of human life. In His divine nature, He was, and always remained, fully God. But in His

humanity, He took on the constraints of time, space, and experience that are part of what it means to be human.

J.B. Lightfoot's insight that the *Logos* "stripped Himself of the insignia of majesty" further clarifies. As Jesus, He did not abandon His divine essence but chose to live without the outward marks of divine glory. He did not cling to the prerogatives of His attributes—omniscience, omnipotence, and omnipresence—choosing instead to live as a servant, fully reliant on the Father for His words, actions, and knowledge. The humility of this decision is staggering: the eternal God, who created all things, subjected Himself to the limitations of a human body, living in complete dependence on His Father.

2. The Divine and Human Coexist in a Single Person

The key to understanding the nature of Jesus is not a division of His two natures but the inseparable union of both the divine and the human in one person. As J.B. Phillips emphasized in his translation of Philippians 2, Jesus, *"who had always been God by nature,"* did not grasp onto His equality with God. Rather, He chose to become a servant, a slave—fully human and fully reliant on the Father. The *Logos* added humanity to His divinity in a manner that does not diminish the fullness of either nature.

This dual nature of Jesus—divine and human—was not a blending or confusing of the two. Rather, it was the seamless coexistence of both natures in the person of Jesus. The fullness of God was present in Jesus, but He did not exercise that fullness. He voluntarily self-limited. While He retained His divinity, He voluntarily laid aside the prerogatives of His divinity and became a human being. He experienced hunger, fatigue, sorrow, and death—all the realities of the human experience. He relied on the Father for everything—what He knew, what He said, what He did.

Yet, He remained fully God. This is the mystery of the incarnation—the *Logos* who was eternal, separate from the Father, and was God became flesh and dwelt among us (John 1:14).

3. Prerogatives and Privileges: The Sovereign Choice to Limit

In the Garden of Gethsemane, when Jesus, faced with the anguish of the coming cross, declared that He could call on twelve legions of angels, He revealed the vast extent of His self-limitation. The Son of God had at His disposal an unimaginable army of angels, yet He chose not to use that power. Instead, He laid aside the privilege of divine intervention for the sake of fulfilling His redemptive mission. His refusal to act in His own defense was a clear demonstration of His voluntary restraint and the sovereign choice to fulfill the Father's will. This choice was not a failure of power but the ultimate demonstration of sacrificial love and obedience.

The restraint Jesus showed in the Gethsemane moment emphasizes His understanding of His mission and His full submission to the will of the Father. It is a profound mystery—the same hands that created the universe, the same voice that spoke life into existence, would allow Himself to be arrested, mocked, and crucified. Yet this was the path He chose, and He walked it with a voluntary surrender, not out of weakness, but in the exercise of perfect strength.

4. The Transfiguration: A Glimpse of Glory

While Jesus' glory was veiled throughout His earthly ministry, the Transfiguration offers a momentary lifting of that veil. As Matthew records, Jesus' face shone like the sun, and His clothes became dazzling white. For a brief moment, His divine glory was revealed to a select few—Peter, James, and John. This fleeting glimpse of His divine nature affirms that Jesus, though He lived as a man, was and always remained fully God.

The Transfiguration was not a contradiction to His humanity but a revelation of the truth of His being. His glory was hidden in His life on earth, but it would one day be fully revealed after His resurrection and ascension. The Transfiguration thus becomes a powerful symbol of the reality of His divinity—an essential truth that undergirds the entire narrative of His life and ministry.

5. Theological Implications: A Model for Humanity

Jesus' self-limitation has profound theological implications. He serves as the ultimate model for humanity—not in spite of His limitations, but precisely because of them. Jesus' life demonstrates what it means to live in complete surrender to the Father. He embraced the full human experience, with all its limitations, and lived in total reliance on God. He demonstrated what it means to live in submission, to trust fully in the Father's will, to model servant leadership.

This understanding of Jesus invites us to reflect on our own relationship with God. Like Jesus, we are called to surrender our own prerogatives, to live with the recognition that our lives are not our own but are given to us for a higher purpose. In our humanity, we are invited to follow the model of Christ, living in reliance on the Father, just as He did.

Conclusion

In the mystery of the incarnation, the *Logos* chose to take on human limitations without surrendering His divinity. He became fully human, experiencing all the constraints of life, but never once losing His divine essence. This self-limitation was a voluntary choice to experience life as we do, for the sake of our redemption. In Jesus, we find the perfect model of what it means to live in full surrender to the will of the Father, fully dependent on Him for everything.

Reflections

1. How does the model of the *Logos* becoming flesh challenge the way we think about Jesus? How does it inform our concepts of strength, humility, and dependence on God?

2. The Transfiguration lifted the veil to give a glimpse of Jesus' hidden, restrained glory. Why would we state that this was the only exception to Jesus living totally as a human being?

3. What moments in your own life have you had a "veil" lifted—revealing something deeper about God's presence or power?

12

The Mind of Jesus, the Christ

The Son of God, eternally exalted, stood at the precipice of the world's most profound mystery: He, the *Logos* who existed with the Father before time, would step into the temporal world and experience the full range of human existence. The Incarnation was not a matter of disguise or pretense, but of self-limitation—a voluntary restriction of divine prerogatives in order to experience life as a human, fully dependent on the Father.

When the *Logos* took on flesh, He was not diminished in essence. His divinity was not laid aside, but certain aspects of divinity—omniscience, omnipotence, and omnipresence—were self-imposed restraints. From the moment of His birth, He chose to live within the confines of human experience: navigating the frustrations of limited knowledge, the vulnerabilities of a body subject to suffering, and the limitations of being bound by time and space.

As He walked among men, Jesus did not wield His divine power as a tool for self-glorification. Instead, He surrendered His will to the Father's, demonstrating perfect humility and utter reliance on God. His self-limitation is most profoundly seen in His prayers, His choices, and in moments of suffering where His full divine authority could have summoned immediate relief, but He chose instead to obey the Father's will.

One of the most telling moments of this self-limitation comes during His prayer in the Garden of Gethsemane. Here, Jesus' plea to the Father—*If it is possible, let this cup pass from Me*—illustrates the depth of His humanity. But the restraint of His divine nature is equally evident when He surrenders to the Father's will: *Neverthe-*

less, not My will, but Yours be done. Even though He had the power to summon twelve legions of angels to deliver Him, He chose the path of obedience to the Father's plan.

"The Veil of Glory"

He who spoke and worlds began,
Now walks in flesh, a humble man.
No throne or crown, no regal might
Only the humble, lowly night.

In Bethlehem, the King was born,
But not adorned in golden form.
His hands, though mighty, clasped in prayer,
He bore the weight of every care.

The *Logos* clothed in human frame,
Not losing power, but setting aim—
To show the world the Father's will,
And humble hearts His love to fill.

In Gethsemane, He knelt in grief,
The cup of suffering, beyond belief.
With angels waiting at His side,
He chose to suffer, not to hide.

Each power divine He chose to stay,
His will surrendered, night and day.
The Prince of glory, veiled in flesh,
Revealed the depth of love made fresh.

Analysis:

In Philippians 2:5-11, a hymn of the early church, the mystery of the Incarnation is revealed. They sang their theology. In the hymn, we are confronted with the paradox of divine self-limitation. Jesus, the eternal Word made flesh, did not cease to be God when becoming a man; He simply chose not to exercise certain divine prerogatives. This is the essence of *kenosis*—the laying aside, not of His nature, but of His rights and privileges as sovereign Lord of the universe.

Theologians have long debated how this self-limitation should be understood, but what is clear in the text is that Jesus did not lose His divinity; rather, He constrained it. He who created all things became subject to time, space, and human frailty. He chose to live a life marked by dependence and humility, taking on the role of a servant, not as one who demands honor, but as one who serves.

The narrative of Jesus' self-limitation stands in stark contrast to the human desire for power and control. From the very beginning of His ministry, He rejected the opportunity to dominate. In the wilderness, when Satan tempted Him with the promise of earthly power, Jesus refused, not because He lacked authority but because He was determined to fulfill the Father's will and plan, no matter the cost.

In His life and teachings, Jesus continually exemplified a radical dependence on God the Father. He prayed without ceasing, asked for guidance, and never acted independently of the Father's will. Even in the moment of His greatest agony, in Gethsemane, when He had the power to escape, He chose obedience, saying, *"Not My will, but Yours be done."* This submission to the Father's will, despite the suffering He knew would come, shows the depth self-limitation.

The Transfiguration (Matthew 17:1-8) offers a rare glimpse into the unfiltered glory of Jesus, reminding us that His glory was veiled during His earthly life. But even in His moment of revelation, Jesus returned to His role as a servant. His purpose was not to be served but to serve and to give His life as a ransom for many. This voluntary restraint of His divine power—the choice to limit Himself to human experience—was the ultimate act of love, demonstrating the nature of God's Kingdom.

Through the lens of Philippians 2:5-11, we are challenged to reconsider our understanding of greatness. In the world, greatness is often associated with power, knowledge, and control, but in the Kingdom of God, true greatness is found in humility, servanthood, and self-sacrifice. Jesus exemplified this Kingdom value through His self-limitation—showing that the path to glory is through surrender, and the path to the Father is through complete obedience.

This self-limitation is not only a theological truth but a practical model for how we are to live as disciples of Jesus. The more we reflect on His humility, His voluntary surrender of power, and His deep trust in the Father's plan, the more we are called to live in similar humility. Jesus, fully God and fully man, shows us that the power of the Kingdom is displayed in weakness, that divine sovereignty is exercised through submission, and that true greatness is found in serving others rather than ruling over them.

The theological implications of Jesus' self-limitation are vast. At the heart of this doctrine lies the mystery of the incarnation: how the divine and human natures of Christ exist together without conflict or division. His choice to live within the constraints of human existence, without relinquishing His divinity, affirms both the reality of His humanity and the fullness of His divinity. We must hold both in tension, recognizing that the God who became flesh did not abandon His sovereignty but exercised it in a way that confounded human expectations—through love, humility, and obedience.

In summary, Jesus' self-limitation is the foundation of His redemptive mission. Through it, He showed us that the way to eternal glory is not through self-exaltation, but through self-emptying. His life and death reveal the heart of the Kingdom of God: a place where greatness is defined not by power, but by sacrifice and service. This understanding challenges us to reassess our own lives, to embrace a Christlike humility, and to live in the freedom of knowing that our Savior is both fully God and fully human, and that in His self-limitation, He became the perfect model for how we should live.

Reflections

1. Why do you think the early church expressed theology through worship? How does this affect your view of worship today?
2. What part of Jesus' self-limitation most challenges the way we think about greatness and strength?

13

The Birth of Jesus

The birth of Jesus is a remarkable and deeply significant event, one that brims with profound layers of transcendence, divine orchestration, and quiet humility. Everything from the sovereignty of God moving the heart of Caesar Augustus, to the miraculous timing of the virgin birth, to the coming together of prophecy, human history, and the humble manger. The grandeur, the depth, and the unexpected nature of this moment in time mark this pivotal event in human history.

The Birth of Jesus: The Sovereign Hand Behind History
Luke 2:1-7

It was no accident that a Roman emperor, Caesar Augustus, issued a decree to take a census of the entire Roman world. This seemingly mundane, governmental action would turn out to be part of a divine plan that had been set in motion long before the emperor's rise to power. In his arrogance, Caesar thought he was making the decision. But behind his decree was the hand of the Almighty, the *"Ancient of Days,"* whose sovereignty reaches over time, space, and all human affairs. His will cannot be thwarted, not even by rulers of empires.

How long would it take to send a word through the vast empire, stretching from the British Isles to the Mesopotamian plains? The decision for all to be taxed, and for Joseph and Mary to travel 90 miles to Bethlehem—this was no small feat in those days. And yet, in God's perfect timing, it was precisely at this moment that Mary, nearing the end of her pregnancy, would travel with Joseph. It was, after all, the fulfillment of prophecy: from Bethlehem would come the ruler of Israel.

And as God moved upon Augustus to send a decree that would move Mary and Joseph to the exact place and time required, it was all part of the eternal plan to bring forth the Savior of the world. What seemed like an ordinary census was the hand of God orchestrating human history for His divine purpose.

"The Sovereign Decree of Caesar Augustus"

A king commands from Rome's great throne,
A census called—all must go home.
From empire's heart, so far and grand,
A ruling spread through every land.
The emperor thought his voice held sway,
But God's own hand moved all that day.
For through this law, His plan took flight—
To bring the Savior into light.
The path was set, the road made clear,
To Bethlehem, God would draw near.
No chance, no fluke, no mortal plan—
God's sovereign will directing man.

The Virgin Birth: A Miracle of Timing and Divine Precision
Luke 2:6-7

The child was about to be born, and the timing could not have been more precise. For months, Mary had carried this sacred burden, and though her journey to Bethlehem may have been arduous—riding on a donkey for days with a child about to be born—it was all part of the grand design. God, in His sovereignty, had chosen the moment, the place, and the person.

In the quiet of the night, under the vast expanse of the heavens, Mary gave birth to the Son of God. It was natural and miraculous. The One who had created the heavens and the earth, who had spoken all things into existence, chose to come in the form of a helpless infant. This child, wrapped in swaddling clothes, would one day wear a crown of thorns. This child, lying in a manger, would one day rule the nations. And in this very moment, the Creator entered into His own creation—entering not with power, but with humility.

"The Virgin Conception and Journey to Bethlehem"
A maiden's womb, untouched by man,
Bore the mystery of God's eternal plan.
The Holy Spirit moved in grace,
And brought a Savior to this place.
In the hush of night, upon a beast's back,
Mary rode through the rocky track.
Ninety miles of dust and stone,
Carrying the weight of the world alone.
In Bethlehem's humble stall, time would come,
For God to walk among us, promised Son.
A mother's labor, a quiet sigh—
The King of kings 'neath starlit sky.

Joseph: The Chosen Caretaker
Matthew 1:18-25
The timing was also perfect in the selection of Joseph as the earthly father of Jesus. A man of righteousness, just in his heart and in his ways, Joseph was chosen not only as the protector of Mary and the child but as the one who would care for and raise the Messiah. Born in Bethlehem, Joseph had to make the journey with Mary, the mother of his child, in fulfillment of the prophecy in Micah 5:2. It was no accident that Joseph came from Bethlehem, as the census would require.

"Joseph: The Chosen Caretaker"
In quiet strength, a man was called,
To guard the Christ, though all seemed small.
A carpenter by trade, his hands had built,

Yet in his heart, the mystery was spilt.
Joseph, obedient to dreams divine,
Took Mary as his wife, by God's design.
He would protect, he would provide,
The earthly father at God's side.
Not of his blood, but chosen, he was true,
To guide the Son, with all he knew.
In Bethlehem's night, the world would see,
Humble guardian of Eternity.

Micah's Prophecy

The prophecy, written over 700 years earlier by the prophet Micah, declared: *"But you, O Bethlehem Ephrathah, who are too little to be among the clans of Judah, from you shall come forth for me one who is to be ruler in Israel, whose coming forth is from of old, from ancient days." Micah 5:2*

That Micah's prophecy would come to pass so precisely is another testament to God's sovereignty over human history. The *"Ancient of Days,"* the One who is above time, had planned every detail of this moment, even the birthplace of His Son. The village of Bethlehem, so small and unremarkable, was chosen to be the birthplace of the greatest King to ever walk the earth.

"Micah's Prophecy: Fulfilled in Bethlehem"

In Bethlehem, so small and low,
A king was born, the world to know.
Though Judah's town was known to few,
A ruler's heart would bring it new.
Ancient words of prophets told,
A king would rise, the story old.
Through time and space, God's plan unfolds,
A ruler, Shepherd—humble, bold.
From ages past, the path was clear,

To bring salvation, to draw near.
Bethlehem, too small for kings of earth,
Yet holds the Child of eternal worth.

The Manger: A Humble Setting for the King
Luke 2:7
And so, in the most unexpected of places—an animal stall, probably nestled within a shallow cave or rocky outcrop in the hills surrounding Bethlehem—God's Son was born. The King of kings, the Lord of the universe, came not into a palace or royal chamber, but to a place where animals fed and slept. It was humble, it was lowly, it was unexpected. God, in His infinite wisdom, did not choose the wealth and grandeur of the world, but instead came in a way that would confound the wise, that would turn the world's expectations upside down. His Kingdom would not be built on power and pride but on humility, service, and sacrifice.

"The Manger: A Humble Setting for the King"
In a humble stall, beneath the sky,
A child was born, the King on high.
No gilded crib, no throne of gold,
But in a manger, rough and cold.

The heavens watched, the earth stood still,
As time itself bent to God's will.
In Bethlehem's hills, so far away,
God's Son lay in the hay.

No palace doors to greet the King,
No banners raised, no songs to sing.
But animals knelt, in silent awe,
At the child who'd fulfill all law.

No crown of jewels, no royal gown,
Just in humble cloth, the King laid down.

The Mighty came, but not with power,
To bring salvation in that hour.

The world's great ones would never see
The glory wrapped in humility.
For this Kingdom, made by grace,
Would not be found in the world's embrace.

From manger low, to cross on high,
The King would reign, the Lamb would die.
In humble form, God's love unfurled,
A King who came to save the world.

The Shepherds: The First to Hear the Good News
Luke 2:8-20

It was to the humble shepherds—outcasts in the eyes of society—
that the first announcement of the birth of the Savior was made.
While the rich and powerful slept in their beds, the lowly shepherds
were the first to be drawn into this extraordinary moment.

Suddenly, the night sky was split open with glory, as a multitude of heavenly hosts appeared, praising God and announcing
peace on earth. *"Glory to God in the highest, and on earth peace,
goodwill toward men."* The shepherds, in awe and wonder, made
their way to the stable and found the child, just as the angels said.

The significance of this moment cannot be overstated. The Savior was not born to the mighty or the wealthy, but to the humble and
lowly. And those who were the most open to hearing the Good
News were the ones who had no power, no wealth, no status—just
hearts ready to receive the message.

"The Shepherds and the Heavenly Host"

Out in the fields, by firelight's glow,
Shepherds kept watch, as the cold winds blow.
The night was quiet, the stars above,
Until the sky broke with heavenly love.

An angel appeared, a radiant light,
Announcing peace, dispelling night.
"Do not be afraid," the angel said,
"For a Savior's born—just as God said."
A multitude of angels filled the sky,
Singing glory, their voices high.
"Glory to God, peace to men,
The Savior is born, the Lord. Amen."

Mary's Heart: A Mother's Pondering

Luke 2:19

As the shepherds returned, glorifying and praising God, Mary kept all these things and pondered them in her heart. What a weight, what a deep, sacred weight this mother carried. She knew, in part, the significance of the child she held in her arms, but in the quiet of the night, she pondered more. She would reflect on the words of the angel Gabriel, the message of Simeon, and the prophecy of Micah. She would ponder the glory of the heavenly host and the visit of the shepherds. But above all, she would carry in her heart the deep mystery that this child was born to die—for the salvation of the world.

"Mary's Pondering Heart"

In the stillness of that sacred night,
Mary held the child, in soft moonlight.
The shepherds came, the angels sang,
And yet her heart, so full, did hang.
She pondered all that had been told,
The songs of angels, the prophecies bold.
The miracle of her newborn Son,
The path ahead, already begun.
Though her heart swelled with wonder,
She knew the weight that lay under.
This child, so small, would soon grow tall,
And her heart, one day, would break for all.

The Christmas Story: A Babe Came to Die

The Christmas story is one of contradiction—of majesty and humility, of transcendence and nearness, of a Savior born to die. This baby, so fragile and helpless, would one day break the chains of sin and death. And His mother, though filled with wonder at the birth of her Son, would one day watch Him die a cruel death, knowing that in His sacrifice, the salvation of the world would be won.

The birth of Jesus in Bethlehem was the turning point in human history. The promises of God, written across centuries, were fulfilled in a child lying in a manger. And as the heavens declared His glory, the earth, though unaware, was set on a course that would change everything.

Analysis: The Tapestry of the Nativity

The birth of Jesus is a rich tapestry of divine sovereignty and human vulnerability, woven together with threads of unexpectedness that challenge every preconceived notion about God's ways. From the Roman emperor's decree to the humble manger, every detail of this story unveils the paradoxes of God's Kingdom—how He works through history, fulfills ancient prophecies, and yet chooses the lowly and the ordinary to bring about the extraordinary.

- **The Sovereign Decree of Caesar Augustus** reminds us that God is sovereign over the affairs of nations. Caesar Augustus, with all his imperial power, unknowingly played a pivotal role in God's plan. His decree moved Mary and Joseph to Bethlehem, fulfilling prophecy and ensuring that the Messiah would be born in the very place foretold by Micah. This detail highlights the transcendence of God, who can move the hearts of kings and rulers to accomplish His purposes.

- **The Virgin Conception and Journey to Bethlehem** emphasize both the miraculous and the ordinary in God's redemptive plan. The divine conception of Jesus in Mary's womb defies human expectations, and yet the journey to Bethlehem was rooted in the everyday struggles of life—long travels, difficult terrain, and the mundane realities of human existence. In this convergence of the supernatural and the natural, God's plan unfolds.

- **Joseph's Role as Caretaker** is a reminder that God often calls unlikely individuals to fulfill crucial roles in His Kingdom. Joseph, a simple carpenter, was chosen to be the earthly father of Jesus. His quiet obedience and faithfulness reflect the kind of leadership God values—not power, prestige, or wealth, but humble, faithful stewardship of God's plan.

- **The Prophecy of Micah** is an echo from the distant past, a proclamation that God's Kingdom would not be established through earthly grandeur but through humility. Bethlehem, small and overlooked, becomes the birthplace of the eternal King. The contrast between the humble setting and the glorious event mirrors the unexpected nature of the Kingdom Jesus would inaugurate.

- **The Shepherds and the Heavenly Host** encapsulate the theme of God's Kingdom being revealed to the humble and the lowly first. The shepherds, often considered outcasts, were the first to hear the Good News, and their joy is the joy of all who hear and believe. The heavenly host's praise magnifies the significance of the birth—this child is not just for Israel, but for all humanity. The announcement to the shepherds marks the inclusive nature of the Kingdom of God.

- **Mary's Heart of Pondering** symbolizes the deep mystery of the Incarnation. As a mother, Mary understood the depth of this miracle, yet she also held the quiet knowledge that her Son's mission would lead to sacrifice. Her pondering heart is an invitation for all of us to reflect on the mystery of Christ's birth, life, and ultimate purpose.

Together, these events reflect the profound depth of the Christmas story. It is a narrative that reveals God's sovereignty over time and history, His surprising choice of humble instruments to fulfill His plan, and the unexpected nature of the Kingdom of God. This is the story of God becoming flesh to redeem humanity, and it challenges every human expectation of what greatness and power truly mean. From the humble manger to the glory of the heavenly host, the birth of Jesus invites us into a Kingdom that upends all our ideas of how God works in the world.

The grandeur and the quietness of the Christmas story, woven together with the spiritual, historical, and emotional elements make it such a profound event in human history. It captures the transcendence of God in orchestrating the details, the sovereignty of His plan, and the unexpected nature of the arrival of the Messiah.

Reflections

1. The decree of Caesar Augustus seems political and mundane, yet it was used by God to fulfill prophecy. What does this suggest about how God works through world events today—even those that seem far removed from spiritual concerns?

2. The birth of Jesus took place in obscurity, not in grandeur. How does the humility of the setting challenge the way we expect God to show up in our own lives?

3. Joseph and Mary stepped into a divine plan that neither of them fully understood. What can their faithfulness teach us about obedience when God's plan isn't fully visible?

4. The first to hear the news of the Messiah's birth were shepherds —social outsiders. What does this say about who God entrusts with His message, and how does that affect the way we view status or worth in the Kingdom?

5. Mary pondered the events of Jesus' birth in her heart, holding both joy and mystery. How might we learn to carry the story of Christmas in a way that invites deeper reflection rather than quick celebration?

14

The Mission in a Name

The passage from Matthew 1:18–25 offers a profound and often overlooked glimpse into the character of Joseph. In this moment, Joseph stands at a crossroads of emotion and decision. His fiancée, Mary, is pregnant, and he knows he is not the father. Under Jewish law, this could have been grounds for a public disgrace or even stoning. But Joseph, a just man, did not want to bring shame upon Mary, and so he resolved to divorce her quietly. He was a man of integrity, his heart moved by compassion rather than indignation.

Before the angel spoke, Joseph was wrestling with more than confusion—he was facing a personal crisis. He had dreams of building a family, of respect in the community, of a marriage grounded in trust. And suddenly, Mary was pregnant, and he knew he wasn't the father. By every cultural expectation and legal precedent, he could have brought her shame, even demanded her punishment. But Joseph, though heartbroken, was also merciful. His decision to divorce her quietly reflects a heart already aligned with the deeper justice of God—not one of retribution, but of grace.

When the angel appeared, Joseph's choice to believe was no small thing. He trusted a dream—something intangible and easy to dismiss. He believed that Mary was telling the truth, that God was doing something bigger than either of them could understand. And he stepped into that mystery, not with fanfare or proclamation, but with quiet, steadfast obedience.

Joseph becomes a kind of model disciple—he listens, obeys, protects, and provides. He is entrusted with the earthly care of the Son of God, not because of power, but because of character. His silent strength shaped Jesus' early life, and his example still speaks today: sometimes the greatest acts of faith are done in silence, behind the scenes, for the sake of love and trust in God's purposes.

Yet it is here that an angel appears to Joseph in a dream, delivering a message that would change the course of his life and the history of the world: *"Do not fear to take Mary as your wife, for that which is conceived in her is from the Holy Spirit."* The angel then gives Joseph the name to call the child: *Jesus, for He will save His people from their sins.* In this moment, Joseph's obedience to God's word was paramount, and his willingness to take Mary as his wife and raise the child as his own demonstrates a radical faith in the unseen work of God.

The angel's message, which echoes the prophecy in Isaiah 7:14, emphasizes not just the miraculous birth of the child but the divine purpose behind it. The name "Jesus," meaning *"The Lord saves,"* declares the very essence of His mission—salvation. This child was not only a miraculous gift but the fulfillment of the deepest need of humanity, to be saved from sin. In this simple act of naming, the mission of Jesus is declared: God's presence with us, in the person of Jesus, is our salvation.

"The Mission in a Name"
In the quiet of a dream-lit night,
A man of faith, in troubled plight,
Heard the angel's voice, serene and clear,
"Take her as your wife; do not fear."
His world, undone by doubt and strife,
Was now restored by God's own life.
For in her womb, a child divine,
The Savior of the world would shine.
No earthly power could thwart His stay,
For God had sent Him as the Way.
This child, so tender, small, and pure,

Would save His people, hearts secure.
The name He bore, a sacred sign,
Jesus, the Lord, the one divine,
To save His people, lost in sin,
Draw them near, make them whole again.
Through blood and tears, He'd pave the way,
To guide the hearts that went astray.
A man named Joseph, humble, just,
Believed in God, in whom he'd trust,
He took the child, and in His name,
The world he knew, no more the same.
For in the mission of this birth,
The Savior came to heal the earth.

The significance of Joseph's role in the birth narrative cannot be overstated. His faith, courage, and willingness to follow the angel's command reveal the depth of his character. In a time when his world could have crumbled around him due to Mary's pregnancy, he chose the path of grace over shame. His obedience to God, despite the cultural and personal cost, highlights an essential aspect of the Kingdom of God: a willingness to obey God's will, even when it doesn't align with societal expectations or personal understanding.

In this passage, the name, "Jesus" encapsulates the mission of the Christ. Matthew highlights that the very name, "Jesus" (meaning *"The Lord saves"*), carries with it the purpose for which the child was born: to save His people from their sins. This is the crux of the Gospel message—salvation is not an abstract concept, but a person, a living, breathing reality in the form of the Son of God. Jesus is not just a symbol of God's presence, as the child in Isaiah's prophecy, but He is the presence of God Himself, dwelling among us, with the explicit mission of bringing salvation.

Matthew's use of Isaiah's prophecy of Immanuel, *"God with us,"* underscores the divinity of Jesus. The difference between the child in Isaiah's time and the child in Mary's womb is that Jesus is not just a symbol of God's presence—He *is* God's presence. His mission was not to merely point to God's deliverance but to be the embodiment of it. Through His life, death, and resurrection, Jesus fulfills the promise of salvation to all who believe.

Joseph's part in this narrative, as one who named the child, is symbolic of the broader call of the Kingdom. Just as Joseph was obedient in naming Jesus, citizens of the Kingdom are called to live according to the values that Jesus embodied—obedience, faith, grace, and ultimately, the mission of salvation. The name of Jesus is not just a label but a declaration of the reality that God's Kingdom has come to earth in the person of Jesus Christ. In following Him, we too are invited into this mission to save, to heal, and to restore.

Reflections

1. Joseph could have responded with anger, but he chose quiet mercy. What does this tell us about how God values inner character over outward appearance?

2. Joseph believed the word of the angel—without proof. How do we discern and respond when God calls us to step into something that defies logic?

3. Joseph's role is often overlooked. Why do you think God entrusted such a critical role to a man who remains mostly in the background?

4. The name "Jesus" means "*The Lord saves.*" How does this name shape your understanding of who Jesus is—not just historically, but personally?

15

Presentation: Simeon and Anna
(Luke 2:25-38)

Two figures stand as witnesses to the fulfillment of God's promises regarding the Messiah: Simeon and Anna. These two individuals are not mentioned in the other Gospel accounts, yet they each play a pivotal role in the recognition of the infant Jesus as the long-awaited Savior. Both of them lived in Jerusalem, and both were part of the faithful remnant who awaited God's redemption for Israel.

Simeon is described as a man who was *"righteous and devout,"* waiting for the *"consolation of Israel"*—the coming Messiah. He had been promised by the Holy Spirit that he would not die before seeing the Christ. Guided by the Spirit, he entered the temple on the day Mary and Joseph brought Jesus to be presented to the Lord.

Upon seeing Jesus, Simeon knew immediately that this child was the Messiah. He took Jesus in his arms and praised God with joy, declaring that he had now seen the salvation God had prepared for all people. His words, often referred to as the *Nunc Dimittis* (Latin for *"Now let depart"*), recognized Jesus as a light for revelation to the Gentiles and the glory of Israel. Simeon also prophesied that Jesus would be a sign that would be opposed and that Mary's heart would be pierced with sorrow because of the path her son would take.

Anna, a prophetess and devout widow, had spent the majority of her long life in the temple, dedicated to prayer and fasting, eagerly awaiting the redemption of Israel. She was in her early eighties, and when she saw Jesus, she too recognized Him as the promised Messiah. Like Simeon, Anna gave thanks to God and spoke about the child to all who were looking for the redemption of Jerusalem. Her words emphasize the hope that Jesus brought, not just for Israel, but for all those who were awaiting God's salvation.

This event takes place within a larger framework of national longing. Israel had endured centuries of foreign occupation and silence from the prophets. Yet a faithful remnant remained— watching, praying, waiting. The expectation surrounding the coming Messiah ran deep, and Simeon and Anna represent those who kept that hope alive. They saw not just a baby, but the fulfillment of divine promise.

That Jesus was presented at the Temple as an infant, and would return decades later to teach and confront religious leaders in the same sacred space, gives a powerful bookend to His earthly ministry. In both moments—cradled in arms and later standing in authority—Jesus reveals the heart of the Father. What began in hushed awe would end in bold proclamation.

And what did Simeon and Anna see that day? A sleeping infant, wrapped and carried like any other. No halo, no majesty—only faith could reveal what flesh concealed. Their vision invites us to ask: do we recognize God's work when it comes to us in such quiet, fragile form?

Together, Simeon and Anna represent the faithful who were living in anticipation of God's promise being fulfilled. Their recognition of Jesus is a testament to the Spirit's work in revealing God's purposes, and their declarations underscore the significance of Jesus' birth, marking the beginning of God's redemptive work for all people.

"Simeon and Anna's Song: Fulfillment and Hope"
Simeon:
At last, O Lord, Your servant's eyes have seen
The promise made to those who dreamed,
A Light to guide, heal, save, and lead,

For all the world, for Israel—You came.
A child so small, mighty in Your grace,
With heart full; now let me leave this place.
For You will be the glory of Your own,
The hope of nations, to Gentiles shown,
Many turn against, some will fiercely fight,
You'll pierce the hearts seeking Your light.
And Mary, dear, your heart will break,
But it is not just for your sake.

Anna:
A lifetime spent in prayer, in hopes divine,
My heart has waited for this holy sign.
And now, eyes behold, voice proclaims,
The Savior comes—Your name acclaimed.
I too, rejoice, for all that we have sought,
Is here, in Him, the one salvation brought.
I lift my voice—Praise for what is done,
His promise kept, His victory begun.
Tell the world, the waiting is no more,
Christ, the Lord, opened heaven's door.

Luke captured the profound faith and recognition that Simeon and
Anna experienced when they saw Jesus. Though coming from different backgrounds—Simeon, a man who received a direct prophecy
from the Spirit, and Anna, a devoted widow of prayer—both individuals shared a common vision. They were both waiting for God's
redemption, and when Jesus arrived, they were filled with joy and
gratitude. Simeon reflects his moment of peaceful fulfillment, while
Anna's voice speaks to the anticipation and joy of all those who
longed for the Messiah.

These two figures can also be seen as symbols of the faithful
remnant, those who held onto the promises of God and waited with

hope for their fulfillment. Their recognition of Jesus marks the first affirmation of Jesus' significance in the world, and their actions highlight the importance of spiritual watchfulness and readiness for God's work in unexpected moments.

In these accounts, we witness Simeon's personal fulfillment and Anna's shared anticipation with all who longed for the Messiah. In them, we see the blending of the recognition of Jesus as the Messiah with the hope for the redemption of all people.

Reflections

1. Simeon and Anna were part of a faithful remnant waiting for God's promises. What does it mean to live in expectation today?

2. How might the example of Joseph and Mary—bringing Jesus to the Temple—reflect a reverence for God's law and a dedication to their child's spiritual life?

3. Why do you think God chose two elderly, faithful people to affirm Jesus' identity rather than the powerful or elite?

4. Simeon and Anna saw only a baby—and yet they believed. What helps you recognize God's work when it comes in small or ordinary ways?

16

The Magi's Visit

The visit of the Magi is one of the most fascinating and mysterious episodes in the early life of Jesus. These wise men, likely scholars and astrologers from the East, had been studying the stars and had come to recognize the extraordinary significance of a new star that appeared in the sky. This star was a sign of the birth of a King—one who was destined to rule not just Israel, but the world. They followed the star, journeying from distant lands, and arrived in Jerusalem with a singular purpose: to worship the newborn King of the Jews.

Their arrival in Jerusalem, however, caused an uproar. The city was shaken by the news that these distinguished visitors were searching for a new king. King Herod, paranoid and insecure about his throne, was deeply disturbed by this news. After consulting with the chief priests and scribes, who revealed that the Messiah was to be born in Bethlehem (according to Micah's prophecy), Herod sent the Magi to find the child. He feigned interest in worshiping the child as well, though in truth he planned to kill the infant to eliminate any threat to his rule.

Guided by the star, the Magi eventually found Jesus in Bethlehem and, overwhelmed with joy, they presented Him with gifts of gold, frankincense, and myrrh—each symbolizing aspects of Jesus' identity as King, God, and Savior. But warned in a dream not to return to Herod, they departed for their own country by another route.

After their departure, an angel of the Lord appeared to Joseph in a dream, instructing him to take Mary and the child and flee to Egypt to escape Herod's wrath. Herod, enraged at being deceived, ordered the massacre of all male children under the age of two in Bethlehem and the surrounding region, a tragic and brutal attempt to rid the world of the "King of the Jews."

This horrific act fulfilled the prophecy in Jeremiah 31:15: "*A voice is heard in Ramah, weeping and great mourning, Rachel weeping for her children; she refuses to be comforted, because they are no more.*" Yet, as the threat was extinguished, another prophetic word was fulfilled—God had called His Son out of Egypt (Hosea 11:1), a symbol of God's ongoing redemptive work in the life of His people.

"The Gifts of the Magi"

Far from lands where sands shift wide,
The Magi journeyed, stars as their guide.
A star had risen, a light so bright,
A King was born—hope pierced the night.
They came with wonder, gifts in hand:
Gold for the King of every land,
Frankincense for the God who reigns,
Myrrh, a sign of One who bears pains.
They found Him there in a humble home,
A small child with grace, not yet grown.
Not in a palace, not in a hall,
But in a house—God with us all.
The joy they felt was deep and pure,
A recognition of love so sure.
But in the shadows, danger grew,
As Herod's fears and madness flew.
A king disturbed by heaven's sign,
His wrath unleashed—no soul was fine.
The cries of mothers, grief unbound,
The silence where no joy was found.
Yet even there, God made a way—

To Egypt's safety, they fled that day.
And when the time had come to rise,
The child returned 'neath Galilee skies.
The gifts they brought would still proclaim
The timeless truth in Jesus' name:
Gold, frankincense, and myrrh they gave
To the child who came to seek and save.

Analysis:

Theological Implications: The visit of the Magi and the gifts they brought speak volumes about the nature of Jesus' mission. Gold, a gift for a king, recognized Jesus' kingship. Frankincense, used in temple worship, acknowledged His divine nature as God incarnate. Myrrh, often used for burial, pointed to the Savior who would die for the salvation of the world. The gifts thus foreshadow the entirety of Jesus' life and work—His kingship, His divinity, and His sacrificial death.

Prophetic Fulfillment: This narrative also involves the fulfillment of multiple prophecies. The Magi's visit and the massacre of the innocents in Bethlehem both fulfill Old Testament scriptures that speak of the Messiah's birth and the suffering associated with it. Herod's violent reaction echoes the rejection and hostility that Jesus would face throughout His life, and the flight to Egypt mirrors the nation of Israel's own history of exile and God's provision during times of danger.

Emotional Tone: This episode evokes a complex emotional response. The joy and wonder of the Magi's visit contrasts sharply with the fear and violence stirred up by Herod. The innocence of the newborn King stands in stark contrast to the wickedness of the ruler who sought to destroy Him. There is an almost tragic beauty in the fulfillment of prophecy—God's redemptive plan unfolding even in the midst of human violence and sorrow.

The Journey of the Holy Family: The flight to Egypt represents both divine protection and a call to trust in God's plan even when the path is difficult and uncertain. Mary, Joseph, and the baby Jesus were not only fleeing an earthly king's wrath but stepping into the broader narrative of God's salvation. The journey to Egypt, and the return from it, echo the larger story of Israel's own exile and return, with Jesus as the true Israelite who fulfills the purposes of God.

These elements—prophecy, fulfillment, and deep theological meaning—are woven into both the joy of the Magi's worship and the sorrow of the massacre, ultimately pointing to God's sovereign plan.

Reflections

1. The Magi brought symbolic gifts to Jesus—gold, frankincense, and myrrh. If you were to bring a gift to Jesus today, what would it be, and why?

2. Herod responded to Jesus' birth with fear and violence, while the Magi responded with worship and joy. What determines whether a heart resists or welcomes God's presence?

3. The Holy Family's journey to Egypt was marked by uncertainty and danger. How do you see God's guidance at work during seasons in your life that feel uncertain or threatening?

4. This story is filled with contrasts: light and darkness, worship and fear, birth and death. Where do you see these tensions playing out in the world today—and how does Jesus' story speak into them?

17

Becoming a Man

The life of Jesus between the age of twelve and thirty is often referred to as the "silent years" in the Gospels, a period where little is recorded. Yet, this silence does not mean passivity. Instead, these years were formative for Jesus, revealing the depth of His humanity. Luke 2:51-52 tells us that during this time, Jesus *"increased in wisdom and in stature and in favor with God and man."* This verse encapsulates the growing process of Jesus as He matured into the man who would later embark on His public ministry.

While the Scriptures offer few specifics, we can imagine the milestones of His life, which reflect His full humanity. Jesus would have learned to walk and talk, grown in understanding, and faced the challenges and trials that come with each developmental stage.

Raised in a Jewish household, He would have been immersed in the customs, traditions, and responsibilities of His faith. He participated in the rhythms of Jewish life—Sabbaths, feasts, prayers, and the study of the Scriptures. His life in Nazareth, a small, tight-knit community, would have offered the normal human experiences of friendship, family, and social interaction.

In the midst of these "ordinary" years, Jesus was not just growing physically and emotionally; He was learning the fullness of obedience to the Father. As the Gospels later show, His will was always in perfect alignment with God's, even in the face of temptation and suffering. This submission to the will of His Father, even in the small decisions of His youth, was a crucial part of His perfect preparation for the sacrificial mission He would one day undertake.

What we see in these years is the human Jesus—the Son of

Man—learning, living, and becoming, without the shortcuts that divine omniscience or omnipotence might have provided. He had to learn like every other human, but His growth was perfectly aligned with God's will. Every challenge He faced, every experience He endured, shaped Him into the Savior the world would need. These "silent years" were not wasted. They were the years of preparation, molding Jesus into the perfect man who could redeem humanity.

"The Silent Years"

In the quiet years, beneath the sky,
A child grew strong, yet none knew why.
He learned to walk, to talk, to play,
He learned the rules that all must obey.

In Nazareth's streets, in humble grace,
He lived a life, none could replace.
He learned the Law, the prayers, the feasts,
In family's care, He found His peace.

But in His heart, a deeper call—
The Son of God, yet man for all.
He learned to serve, He learned to wait,
Each step He took, ordained by fate.

The wisdom grew, the stature climbed,
The perfect man, by God designed.
In silence lived, yet never still,
God's plan was worked, His heart His will.

And though the years seemed lost in time,
Each moment shaped His heart and mind.

The world would know, in fullness bright,
The silent years were shaping Light.

Analysis:

The significance of Jesus' "silent years" cannot be overstated. Theologians have long discussed the tension between the divine and human aspects of Jesus, but the reality of Jesus growing up as a fully human child challenges our perceptions of divinity and incarnation. As the text we reflected upon indicates, Jesus learned, He grew, and He experienced life in a manner that reflects His humanity.

Hebrews 2:9-10 emphasizes that Jesus was *"made lower than the angels"* for a time, tasting death so that through suffering, He could become *"perfect"* for His mission. This perfection was not about moral flawlessness—Jesus was sinless from birth—but rather about being fully prepared, fully equipped to serve as the Savior of mankind. The path He walked was not an easy one. He faced the same growing pains, the same frustrations, and the same temptations that every human faces. And yet, He did so without sin, submitting every part of His life to the will of His Father.

The temptation to "bypass" the human experience in favor of divine intervention is always present, but Jesus, in His self-imposed limitations, did not take that route. He did not jump straight from His birth to His ministry. He lived a full human life, experiencing all the physical, emotional, and spiritual growth that any person would undergo. He learned obedience, not because He was disobedient, but because obedience is a choice—one He made every day. In the small, mundane moments of life—learning carpentry, dealing with family dynamics, attending synagogue—He was being perfected (fitted to the purpose) for the monumental task that lay ahead.

For us, this has profound implications. Jesus didn't just come to die for our sins; He came to live a life that could be held up as the model of humanity at its best. He showed us that being human doesn't mean we are destined to fail or live without hope. His life, from His "silent years" to His public ministry, is the fullest picture of what it means to live according to God's will. His perfection through suffering means that He can identify with us fully, not just as a distant deity but as the man who walked the same path we walk.

The "silent years" are not simply a gap in the historical narrative. They are the quiet foundation upon which the Gospel would stand. In those years, Jesus was becoming the perfect sacrifice, the perfect Savior—truly man, yet perfectly aligned with God's will.

The tension between the human limitations that Jesus chose to embrace and the divine purpose that He was fulfilling has been the subject of speculation since the earliest days of Christianity. The Bible does not debate—it reveals. The "silent years" are a powerful testimony to the fact that Jesus didn't simply appear as a fully-formed Savior. He became one, through experience, obedience, and growth, preparing for the greater work ahead. This deepens our understanding of His humanity and underscores the significance of His incarnation. This does not diminish Him, it elevates Him.

Reflections

1. Jesus chose to grow and learn as we do, without bypassing the human experience. How does this affect your understanding of His ability to relate to your daily struggles?

2. Luke says Jesus grew *"in wisdom and in stature and in favor with God and man."* What might this holistic growth look like in your own life—and how can it become a conscious pursuit?

3. Much of Jesus' preparation for ministry happened in silence, away from public view. How can this encourage us during seasons where our growth feels unseen or unnoticed?

4. Jesus learned obedience through daily life—through work, family, faith, and waiting. Where do you see opportunities for obedience in the "ordinary" parts of your life right now?

5. The poem speaks of "a deeper call" within Jesus. What helps you stay attuned to God's deeper call on your life—even when the path feels slow, hidden, or unfinished?

18

Forerunner of the Kingdom

For four hundred years, the heavens had been silent. No prophet arose in Israel. The last to speak on behalf of God was Malachi, who had foretold the coming of a messenger who would prepare the way for the Lord. But then silence—deep, waiting silence. The people of Israel, under the oppressive rule of Rome, were desperate for the Messiah. And yet, for generations, no voice had broken through the quiet.

Then, out of the wilderness, came John the Baptist, a man clothed in camel's hair with a leather belt around his waist, living a life of asceticism and calling out to the people to repent. His ministry was a stark contrast to the elaborate rituals of the religious leaders. While the priests and Pharisees lived in wealth and power, John stood in the Jordan River, calling the people to humble themselves and be baptized for the forgiveness of sins. His message was one of judgment, purification, and reformation.

Everyone who heard of John, wondered, "Is this the One?" Luke notes their heightened expectations and speculation: *15As the people were in expectation, and all were questioning in their hearts concerning John, whether he might be the Christ, 16John answered them all, saying, "I baptize you with water, but he who is mightier than I is coming, the strap of whose sandals I am not worthy to untie. He will baptize you with the Holy Spirit and fire. 17His winnowing fork is in his hand, to clear his threshing floor and to gather the wheat into his barn, but the chaff he will burn with unquenchable fire (Luke 3:15-17)."*

His voice echoed the words of Malachi: *"I will send my messenger who will prepare the way before me. Then suddenly the Lord you are seeking will come to his temple; the messenger of the covenant, whom you desire, will come,"* (Malachi 3:1). John saw his role clearly—as the prophetic forerunner who would prepare the hearts of the people for the coming of the Messiah, fulfilling Malachi's prophecy.

John's role as the forerunner was not just to baptize with water but to prepare the hearts of the people for the coming of the Messiah. When questioned by the religious leaders, he firmly declared, *"I am not the Messiah,"* but pointed to the One who would come after him, whose sandals he was not worthy to untie.

His entire ministry was a message of readiness—*Repent, for the Kingdom of Heaven has come near.* He did not shy away from confronting the religious leaders, calling them a brood of vipers, demanding that they bear fruit in keeping with repentance. For John, the arrival of the Messiah was not just a spiritual awakening—it was a time of reckoning.

Many saw John's actions and message as the fulfillment of ancient prophecies. He lived a life of ritual purity, much like the Essenes, a group in the wilderness that believed in the imminent coming of the "Son of Light" who would bring judgment and restore righteousness. Whether or not John was directly associated with the Essenes, his message aligned with their apocalyptic vision—the time of reformation had come, and the Messiah was on His way.

As the people came to John in droves, many were ready for a Messiah who would restore Israel's political power. But John's message was a reminder: this was a spiritual kingdom first. The Messiah would come to challenge hearts, not just armies.

"I Am Not the One"
A voice cried out in desert air,
A messenger to clear the way.

"Repent, O Israel, prepare—
Be washed within the stream today."
Clothed in camel's hair, a humble man,
He called the proud to yield their pride:
"The Kingdom comes by God's own plan—
Not for the strong, but those who've cried."
"I am not the One, but He draws near—
The Lamb of God will soon appear."
Both judgment and His grace are near—
But those who turn will see Him clear.

Analysis:

John the Baptist's role as the forerunner to Jesus was not only prophetic but also deeply tied to the expectations of the Jewish people.
His arrival, after 400 years of prophetic silence, was a loud proclamation that the time had come for the Messiah. His baptism symbolized the cleansing of Israel, a physical act that was an outward sign
of the inward repentance required to receive the Kingdom of God.

The expectation of a Messiah during this time was heavily influenced by a long history of oppression and unfulfilled hopes. The
people, including the Essenes, were looking for a political and military ruler to deliver them from Rome's grasp. Yet, John's message, a
blend of judgment and grace, set the tone for a Kingdom that would
defy worldly expectations of power, wealth, or prestige. John's baptism was not an anointing for kingship but an invitation to enter a
radically different Kingdom, one that required humility, repentance,
and an openness to the transformative rule of God.

In his confrontations with the religious authorities, John placed
himself as the intermediary who prepared the way for Jesus. His acknowledgment that he was not the Messiah, but that the Messiah
was coming, is essential to understanding the role of John in relation
to Jesus. Where John's message was one of judgment, Jesus' mission would focus on salvation, grace, and the establishment of a

spiritual Kingdom that would challenge all notions of power and control.

For those who followed John, the transition to following Jesus was not one of rejection but of fulfillment. John's call to prepare the way was answered by Jesus, who brought the fullness of God's Kingdom. John's life and ministry set the stage for the arrival of the Messiah in a way that would challenge the Jewish people's expectations—just as the Kingdom Jesus proclaimed would challenge every human expectation.

Reflections

1. John's voice broke 400 years of silence. How do you think long periods of waiting shape a person's—or a people's—readiness to hear from God?

2. John clearly stated, "*I am not the One.*" Why is it important—even today—for spiritual leaders and followers to know their role in relation to Christ?

3. John expected a Messiah of judgment and power, yet Jesus came with mercy and healing. What does John's eventual doubt (Luke 7:18–23) tell us about how hard it can be to let go of our assumptions—even when we're close to God?

4. Two of John's disciples eventually followed Jesus (John 1:29–37). What helps you know when it's time to shift your focus—from a good thing to the greater thing God is doing?

19

Anointing and Baptism

In the beginning of His public ministry, Jesus' baptism is a moment of divine revelation. As He steps into the Jordan River, He submits to the will of His Father. The skies open, and the Holy Spirit descends upon Him like a dove, while God the Father declares, *"You are my beloved Son; with you I am well pleased* (Mark 1:11)."

This anointing with the descending of the Spirit on Jesus signifies His divine appointment as the King of God's Kingdom. It's a public commissioning for a mission that will extend far beyond what anyone could have anticipated. The presence of the Spirit marks Jesus as the *Anointed One*, the Messiah, whose Kingdom will not be of this world. The Kingdom is inaugurated not through political power but through submission, service, and sacrifice.

Though Jesus is sinless, His baptism is an important moment in "fulfilling all righteousness", aligning Himself with the will of the Father and people He came to save. It is the moment when the eternal plan of redemption moves from promise to fulfillment. His Kingdom will be one of justice, peace, and righteousness, where those who repent and believe will be welcomed as citizens.

Jesus told John, *"It is proper for us to do this to fulfill all righteousness"* (Matt. 3:15). Though the full meaning remains mysterious, it reveals something essential: Jesus was following the prompting of the Spirit. John tried to dissuade Jesus. He knew this man, his cousin. No need for repentance. But for Jesus, it was not about repentance, but about obedience. And what might have been missed had He not obeyed? The heavens opened, the Spirit descended, and the voice of the Father spoke. Obedience—sometimes without full understanding—becomes the doorway to revelation.

"Baptism of the King"

Into the water, the King descends,
Not for His sin, but for ours, He bends.
The dove descends, in light and grace,
Anointing the One to take our place.
The voice of God, in thunder speaks,
"You are My Son, in You I delight."
From humble waters, the King arises,
With Heaven's blessing, to open the skies.
A Kingdom not by sword or might,
But by the Spirit's pure light.
O King of Glory, to You we bow,
The Kingdom's reign begins here, now.

Analysis: The Kingdom Inaugurated through Baptism

Jesus' baptism at the Jordan is the divine anointing that marks the commencement of His reign as the King of God's Kingdom. It is a powerful moment of identification and empowerment. Through this act, Jesus steps into His role as the long-awaited Messiah.

Theologically, His baptism speaks to the foundational truth of the Kingdom of God: it is not one of military conquest or earthly power, but one that is inaugurated through the humble submission of the Son to the Father's will.

The Kingdom of God begins not with a loud declaration of power but in the quiet submission of Jesus to the waters. This moment is a profound statement about the nature of the Kingdom—humble, obedient, and focused on spiritual renewal.

For believers, baptism remains a powerful sign of participation in the Kingdom—symbolizing death to sin and resurrection to new life. Just as Jesus was anointed with the Spirit, so too do believers receive the Holy Spirit upon their faith commitment to God through Jesus (Acts 10:44-48). Paul stressed that this baptism in the Spirit makes us part of the mystical Body of Christ (1 Cor. 12:13). Our act of obedience in water baptism is a proclamation of the gospel and a public testimony of our faith. It portrays the death, burial, and resurrection of Jesus—and our own spiritual death, burial, and resurrection through faith (Roman 6:1-11). Our own baptism marks us as citizens of the Kingdom of God, empowered to live according to the values of God's reign.

The Wilderness and the Temptation

After His baptism, Jesus is led by the Spirit into the wilderness, where He faces the full weight of temptation. For forty days, He fasts and prays. At the end, He is tested by the Adversary, who seeks to derail the mission of the Messiah. The temptations are stark: Jesus is offered political power, material provision, and personal glory.

But each temptation is a challenge to redefine the nature of the Kingdom Jesus came to establish. Jesus' refusal to bow to Satan's offers reaffirms that His Kingdom will not be built through worldly methods or in pursuit of self-interest. Instead, Jesus chooses obedience to the Father, even in the face of hardship, thus laying the foundation for the Kingdom of God, which is characterized by humility, sacrifice, and spiritual victory.

The temptations are not merely a personal trial for Jesus; they are a cosmic battle over the direction of the Kingdom. Jesus' victory in the wilderness signals that His Kingdom will be established through spiritual power, not earthly might.

"Tempted in the Desert"

Alone He stands, the wilderness wide,
No bread to eat, no place to hide.
The tempter comes with promises grand,
"All this can be, if you take my hand."
But Jesus stands, His heart steadfast,
His vision clear—this will not last.
For power gained by force or greed,

Cannot satisfy the soul's true need.
He chooses truth, He chooses love,
A Kingdom not below, but above.
He rejects the world, its fleeting crown,
His Kingdom comes—Thy will come down.

Analysis: The Kingdom Tempted, the Kingdom Revealed

The temptation in the wilderness is a pivotal moment in the life of Jesus. It reveals that the Kingdom of God cannot be understood in terms of power, success, or material wealth as the world sees them. The Kingdom Jesus inaugurates is radically different—it is a Kingdom of humility, where self-sacrifice reigns supreme, not self-promotion.

In rejecting Satan's offers, Jesus affirms the nature of His Kingdom: it will be built through obedience to God's will, not through coercion or manipulation.

For the believer, this moment is a reminder that the Kingdom of God is not a Kingdom of ease or instant gratification. It is a Kingdom where faithfulness, obedience, and trust in God are paramount. The wilderness experience shows that the Kingdom does not come through earthly means but through spiritual perseverance and reliance on God.

Reflections

1. Jesus obeyed the Spirit's prompting to be baptized—even when the full reason wasn't clear. How do you respond when God asks for obedience before understanding?

2. John only recognized Jesus as the Messiah when the Spirit descended (John 1:32–33). What does this teach us about spiritual insight and how God reveals truth?

3. The Father's words in Mark and Luke were spoken directly to Jesus: "*You are My Son... I am pleased.*" What significance might that affirmation have had for Jesus as He stepped into ministry?

20

The Temptations of Jesus
—Testing the Anointed

In the barren wilderness, under the scorching sun, Jesus stood at the crossroads of His identity and destiny. This was the crucible where His resolve would be tested. Forty days in solitude, enduring hunger and isolation, were followed by a confrontation with Satan, who seized upon this moment of weakness to tempt Jesus with three pivotal offers. Each temptation directly challenged the expectations of what the Messiah was supposed to be.

The First Temptation: Stones to Bread

Command these stones to become bread, Satan coaxed. Jesus, weakened by hunger, was offered a shortcut to satisfy His immediate needs. This first temptation challenged His reliance on the Father. The Israelites had long expected the Messiah to provide for their physical needs, like Moses had provided manna in the wilderness. Would Jesus use His messanic power to fulfill desires of the flesh?

But Jesus' response made it clear: *Man shall not live by bread alone, but by every word that comes from the mouth of God.* He rejected the temptation to use His power for personal gain. The Messiah would not serve the people's material desires; He would fulfill a deeper, spiritual hunger. He would offer the bread of life, not just bread for the stomach.

"Stones to Bread"

In the barren wilderness, alone,
The Spirit led Him, weak, unknown,
Forty days with hunger's pangs,
No voice but silence, winds that sang.

The Devil's whisper, soft and sly,
"Turn stones to bread, and satisfy
Your hunger, prove your power—show,
The world, the might of God below."
But Jesus speaks, with steady grace,
"Man does not live by bread's embrace,
But by each word that God has said,
I live, not my will, but His instead."

The Second Temptation: Jump from the Temple

The second temptation carried with it the promise of spectacular awe. Satan took Jesus to the pinnacle of the temple and urged Him to jump, quoting Scripture: *For he will command his angels concerning you to guard you.* This temptation tested whether Jesus would display His divine power to dazzle and convince the crowds. Would He use sensational miracles to win followers, to prove His worth and identity as Messiah?

Once again, Jesus refused. You *shall not put the Lord your God to the test*, He replied. His path was not one of public displays to captivate and impress. Jesus would not win the world through grandiose gestures but through humble obedience. His kingdom was not about miracles to garner fame—it was about service, sacrifice, and obedience to God's will.

"The Temple Jump"

Upon the Temple, high and tall,
Satan beckons, "Prove your call,
Take the leap and angels' wings
Will bear you up, and all will sing!"
But Jesus stands, His eyes aglow,
"Do not test the Lord, and throw
Yourself to fate, for God's design
Is far beyond some reckless sign."

The Third Temptation: All the Kingdoms of the World

Finally, Satan offered Jesus all the kingdoms of the world, a tempting promise of political power and glory. This was the ultimate offer: dominion over all nations, the kind of reign the Jews had long hoped for in their Messiah. Would Jesus claim the authority to rule and conquer in the way the people expected—a military king who would defeat the Romans and restore Israel to its former glory?

Jesus rejected this offer decisively, *You shall worship the Lord your God, and him only shall you serve*. The Messiah would not be a ruler through force and violence, but through love, grace, and sacrificial service. Jesus' kingdom was not of this world; it was spiritual, eternal, and built upon the foundation of worshiping God alone.

"Worldly Power"

A vision vast, the kingdoms' sweep,
Satan offers, "All these to keep,
Bow to me, and they are yours,
The power, the rule, the ancient shores."
But Jesus, firm, with courage speaks,
"Worship only God, whose peaks
Are higher still than all you show,
His kingdom reigns, forevermore."

The Temptations and the Messiah's Path

The wilderness tempted Jesus with shortcuts—quick fixes that promised immediate results but would have led Him astray from the mission set by His Father. These were not just temptations to indulge in power or personal gain; they were tests of His identity as the Messiah. Jesus was being asked to redefine what the Messiah was meant to be, and He chose to follow a radically different path than what was expected by His people.

Each temptation, in essence, confronted the prevailing hopes of the Jewish people: a welfare Messiah who would provide for their material needs, a spectacular Messiah who would dazzle them with signs and wonders, and a political Messiah who would overthrow their enemies and restore Israel's glory. But Jesus rejected all of these. His kingdom was not about meeting earthly desires, but about transforming hearts and minds. It would not come through force or spectacle but through sacrificial love.

Analysis: The Temptations and the Nature of the Kingdom

The Temptation narrative is a pivotal moment that establishes the true nature of the Messiah's mission. Satan's temptations mirror the common Jewish expectations of the Messiah, which were shaped by centuries of oppression and longing for deliverance. The people hoped for a Messiah who would meet their physical needs, perform miracles to validate His divinity, and overthrow the oppressive Roman regime to establish a political kingdom of power and glory.

Jesus' rejection of these temptations marks a definitive break with these expectations. His Messiahship would not be defined by political power, material wealth, or miraculous displays of force. Instead, it would be defined by obedience to the Father's will, by humility, by service, and by a willingness to sacrifice for others.

This rejection of worldly power and glory is a foundational moment in the Gospels. It reveals that Jesus' kingdom is not of this world but is spiritual, eternal, and transformative. His rule would be established not through violence and force, but through grace, forgiveness, and the ultimate sacrifice on the cross.

Reflections

1. How do the temptations of Jesus mirror our own?
2. How do they differ?
3. How does the way Jesus dealt with temptation give a model for how we should resist temptation?
4. Jesus faced the temptation to take shortcuts. Where are you most tempted to "shortcut" God's way for your life?

21

Calling of the First Disciples

The scene unfolds by the Jordan River, where John the Baptist had been preparing the way. John had baptized Jesus, seen the Spirit descend like a dove, saw Jesus depart for the wilderness. After the forty days, John sees Jesus returning and with great humility, points to Him and declares, *"Behold, the Lamb of God who takes away the sin of the world."* Two of John's disciples, Andrew and another unnamed follower (that most believe to be John, the writer of the Gospel), upon hearing John's words are compelled to follow after Jesus. They are seekers—spiritually hungry men standing on the precipice of something new.

Jesus turns to them and asks, *"What are you seeking?"* They ask where He is staying, and with simple invitation, He answers, "Come and see."

In this moment, Jesus begins to take His first steps toward fulfilling His mission—calling others to come into relationship, to come and be part of a different kingdom.

Andrew, recognizing something in Jesus, rushes to find his brother Simon and tells him, *"We have found the Messiah."* Simon is brought before Jesus, and with a gaze, Jesus renames him—Cephas, the rock. They are introduced to something profound, yet they still carry the weight of their own expectations.

The following day, Jesus calls Philip, who, in turn, finds Nathanael. Philip's declaration—*"We have found him of whom Moses and the prophets wrote"*—is met with skepticism. Nathanael, incredulous, responds, *"Can anything good come out of Nazareth?"* But when Nathanael meets Jesus, his doubts are dispelled. Jesus sees him with the eyes of revelation, saying, *"Before Philip called you, I saw you under the fig tree."* Nathanael, overwhelmed, declares, *"Rabbi, you are the Son of God! You are the King of Israel!"*

Though these first disciples are beginning to sense that something extraordinary is unfolding, their messianic expectations still differ—some seek a king who will overthrow Rome, others a teacher with deeper wisdom. Jesus, however, reveals a kingdom far greater than an earthly throne, a kingdom that is present and yet to come.

"The Call of the Lamb"

Beneath the stars, by Jordan's shore,
The Baptist's voice, a call, a roar,
"Behold, the Lamb! The Lamb of God,
Who comes to bear the sinner's load,"
The sin, the weight, the world's despair—
He's here, the One who's answered prayer!"
Two hearts, they hear, and hearts ignite,
A hunger deep, a thirst for Light.
They follow Him, as He walks on,
The path of life, where He is drawn.
"Rabbi," they ask, "Where do You stay?"
"Come, and you'll see," He calls that day.
Andrew runs, his joy to share,
His brother's name his single care,
"We've found the One! The Christ, the King!"
His words, a sweet and hopeful sting.
And Simon's name—he shall be called,
A stone whose faith the Lord installed.
But Christ, the Rock, the truth confessed,
The church's true foundation blessed.
The next day comes with Philip's call—
A Nazarene, whom none could call
Prophet or king, yet in Him see—

The truth unfolding, wild and free.
Nathanael doubts, but soon will find,
The Savior calls, and He is kind.
From fig tree's shade, to heaven's door,
They'll see the angels rise, and soar.
What they want and need will be revealed—
The Lamb, the King, the Christ, the Real.

Analysis:

The calling of the first disciples is not just an introduction to a new teacher, but the beginning of the unveiling of Jesus' true identity. The varied responses and expectations of the disciples—Andrew, Simon, Philip, and Nathanael—reveal the diverse ways in which people of that time understood the Messiah.

Some, like Andrew and Philip, recognize Jesus as the fulfillment of Messianic prophecy and eagerly declare, "We have found the Messiah." However, even these early followers are uncertain about the full nature of His mission and identity. Their expectations of the Messiah were colored by the hopes of a political liberator, a king who would deliver Israel from Roman oppression.

John the Baptist's declaration of Jesus as the *"Lamb of God"* shifts the understanding of the Messiah. Rather than a conquering king in the traditional sense, Jesus is introduced as the sacrificial Lamb who will take away the sins of the world. This Lamb is not just a figure of power and royalty but also one of profound sacrifice and humility. The disciples' early responses, while full of excitement, show that they are still in the process of understanding what kind of Messiah Jesus truly is.

Nathanael's initial skepticism, *"Can anything good come out of Nazareth?"* represents the general disbelief among the Jews regarding a Messiah who would come from such a humble, unexpected place. However, when Jesus reveals His knowledge of Nathanael's actions under the fig tree, Nathanael is convinced. This marks the beginning of a deeper revelation for all of them—not just of Jesus' divine authority, but of the kind of Messiah He will be. Through the simple act of seeing Nathanael under the fig tree, Jesus demonstrates that His kingdom is not one of earthly power but one of divine insight and presence.

The calling of these first disciples also marks the start of the disciples' transformation. They are no longer merely seeking a political Messiah, but a spiritual leader who will lead them into the truth of God's Kingdom. The promise of greater things to come—like the vision of angels ascending and descending on the Son of Man—points to the opening of heaven itself through Jesus.

Thus, this early calling reveals the layers of Messianic expectation, some of which will be shattered, while others will be fulfilled in ways far beyond what any of the disciples could have imagined. The image of the Lamb of God challenges conventional views of Messiahship, revealing that God's Kingdom is not about earthly power, but about sacrificial, redemptive love and divine revelation.

These moments of the first disciples' calling and their varied expectations of the Messiah, invites us to reflect on how initial encounters with Jesus can lead to profound transformation and how Messianic expectations must evolve to truly understand His mission. True for them and true for us.

Reflections
1. The first followers had hopes and assumptions of the Messiah. What were your expectations when you began following Jesus? How have they changed?
2. Several of these disciples met Jesus because someone they trusted pointed the way. What role has friendship or personal testimony played in your journey of faith?
3. Jesus' question to the first two disciples—*"What are you seeking?"*—still echoes today. If Jesus asked you that now, how would you answer?

22

Seven Signs—Jesus was the Christ

The Seven Signs in John's Gospel are powerful and rich with theological meaning. John chose seven events or actions as *semeion* (sign). Each pointing to a deeper reality about who Jesus is and what He came to do. These signs are meant to show Jesus' divine authority and establish Him as the true source of life, offering new creation and restoration to the brokenness of the world.

Given the depth of each sign, we will explore each one individually. But we must keep in perspective the purpose of John in writing his gospel and choosing these particular signs:

Jesus performed many other signs in the presence of His disciples, which are not written in this book. But these are written so that you may believe that Jesus is the Christ, the Son of God, and that by believing you may have life in His name (John 20:30-31).

The larger purpose is revealing of Jesus' glory and divine mission. Since the Seven Signs reveal Jesus' power over creation, sickness, death, and the elements, they reveal His ultimate role as the giver of life and the initiator of a new creation.

The Signs that Speak—Revelation Through Action

The Gospel of John is unique in its structure and presentation of Jesus as the Son of God. Among the most significant aspects of this Gospel are the "Seven Signs" that Jesus performed, each revealing a facet of His divine nature and His purpose in coming to earth. These signs are not merely displays of power; they are profound acts of revelation that call people to believe in Jesus, not just as a teacher or miracle worker, but as the Christ, the Son of God.

1. Changing Water to Wine (John 2:1-11)

The first sign occurs at a wedding in Cana, where Jesus turns water into wine. This miraculous act signifies that Jesus has the authority to transform the ordinary into the extraordinary. It is a sign of the newness that Jesus brings, a picture of the joy and abundance found in the kingdom of God. His power is not only over the natural elements, but it is a symbol of the deeper transformation He offers to the hearts of humanity. (We explored this in the first vignette.)

2. Healing a Royal Official's Son (John 4:46-54)

The second sign reveals Jesus' authority over distance and time. The official's son, sick and near death, is healed by Jesus' mere spoken word. This act shows that Jesus' power is not limited by physical boundaries, demonstrating that He is not just a healer, but the one who holds power over life and death.

3. Healing a Disabled Man (John 5:1-15)

In this sign, Jesus heals a man who had been paralyzed for 38 years. Jesus' act of healing demonstrates His authority to restore wholeness to the brokenness of human life. He offers more than just physical healing; He extends spiritual restoration, showing His ability to heal not just the body but the soul. Notably, the healing was on the Sabbath—a deliberate act challenging tradition and provoking opposition from the Jews. Jesus was not bound by human conventions.

4. Feeding the 5,000 (John 6:1-14)

The miraculous feeding of the 5,000 in the wilderness points to Jesus as the Bread of Life. In the context of the Exodus story, where God provided manna in the wilderness, Jesus shows that He is the true sustenance of life (Jn. 6:32). He contrasts Himself with Moses who satisfied temporarily. Jesus calls Himself the rue bread of heaven: He is the one who satisfies the hunger of the human soul.

5. Walking on Water (John 6:16-21)

In this sign, Jesus walks on water to reach His disciples who are caught in a storm. This miraculous act reveals that Jesus has power over the natural world. This is one of the "nature" miracles. They are some of the more dramatic displays of God's power (Jn 14:10) working through Jesus. His presence with His disciples in the storm reminds us He is with His people in times of trial and uncertainty.

6. Healing a Man Born Blind (John 9:1-12)

In this sign, Jesus heals a man born blind, offering him not just physical sight but also spiritual enlightenment. The healing of blindness is a powerful symbol of Jesus' mission to bring spiritual sight to those who are lost in darkness. Jesus is the Light of the World, and this sign points to His ability to illuminate the hearts and minds of those who are in spiritual blindness.

7. Raising Lazarus from the Dead (John 11:1-43)

The final and most profound sign is the raising of Lazarus from the dead. In this moment, Jesus demonstrates God's power over death itself. Lazarus' resurrection is a sign of the ultimate victory Jesus will have over death through His own resurrection. It foreshadows the new creation that Jesus' death and resurrection will bring about—the defeat of death and the restoration of life.

Each of these signs is a pointer to a deeper reality. The Gospel of John makes clear that these signs are not ends in themselves, but means by which Jesus reveals His role of Messiah and the new creation that He has come to inaugurate through the Kingdom of God. As John writes in chapter 20, *"These are written so that you may believe that Jesus is the Christ, the Son of God, and that by believing you may have life in His name"* (John 20:31). These signs are a call to faith, an invitation to believe in the transformative power of the Christ, the Son of God.

"Signs of the Kingdom"

From water to wine, He made all things new,
A sign of joy, of life made true.
A word from His lips, and death took flight—
A royal son healed by Heaven's might.
A man by the pool, broken and low,
Rose at His word—"Take up your bed, go."
In the desert, He fed with a blessing in hand,
More than bread—He gave the Promised Land.
On the waves, He walked, calm and bold,
The storm grew still at His voice untold.
A blind man saw—his dark made bright,
Touched by the hands of the world's true Light.
And Lazarus' tomb, so cold, so sealed,
Broke at His cry—death's fate repealed.
These signs were more than wonders displayed;
They call us to trust, believe, be saved.
The signs point forward, they point to the King,
To Jesus the Christ, and the new life He brings.
Believe in His power—in Him find your way,
For He is the Light, the Truth, the Way.

Significance of the Seven Signs—New Creation and New Life

The Seven Signs in John's Gospel carry profound theological weight, pointing to Jesus' role as the Messiah and His mission to establish God's kingdom on earth. These signs do not simply demonstrate Jesus' miraculous power; they act as signs that point to a new reality—one that is inaugurated through Jesus, the Christ.

Revelation of Jesus' Divine Authority

Each of the seven signs demonstrates Jesus' authority over creation, time, distance, and even death. From turning water into wine to raising Lazarus from the dead, Jesus is revealed as the Lord who has the power to transform and restore all things. These signs reveal Him as the Christ, affirming that He is not just a prophet, but the very Son of God who comes to bring life and redemption.

A New Creation

The sequence of signs is often interpreted as pointing toward the creation of a new world. In each sign, Jesus is bringing restoration and life to the brokenness of creation—whether through physical healing, the restoration of sight, or the provision of life-giving sustenance. These signs are a foretaste of the new creation that Jesus will bring about through His death and resurrection. His resurrection, in particular, is seen as the ultimate sign of the new creation, where death is defeated and eternal life is offered to all who believe in Him. John consistently reveals that through His death and resurrection, we have life eternal (John 3:16-17).

Invitation to Faith and Life

John's Gospel makes it clear that the purpose of these signs is to bring people to faith in Jesus. By witnessing these signs, the disciples (and all who read this Gospel) are invited to believe that Jesus is the Christ, the Son of God, and by believing, they may have life in His name (John 20:31). The signs are not mere miracles; they are revelatory acts that call for a response of faith. They invite the reader and the observer to step into the new creation that Jesus offers through His life, death, and resurrection.

The Seven Signs, then, are more than a series of miraculous acts. They are acts of revelation, calling people to see Jesus for who He truly is—God's Son, the Messiah, and the bringer of new life. As we reflect on these signs, we are invited to respond in faith and trust in Jesus, the source of all life.

Reflections
Water to Wine (John 2:1–11):
Where in your life do you need Jesus to bring transformation—from emptiness to joy, from ordinary to extraordinary?

Healing the Royal Official's Son (John 4:46–54):
Jesus healed with a word, across distance. How does this sign shape your trust in God's power to work in unseen places and unanswered prayers?

Healing the Disabled Man (John 5:1–15):
Jesus asked, *"Do you want to be healed?"* What broken place in your life is waiting for His restoring touch—and what's your response to His question?

Feeding the 5,000 (John 6:1–14):
Jesus didn't just feed the hungry—He revealed Himself as the Bread of Life. In what ways are you seeking to be filled by things that don't truly satisfy?

Walking on Water (John 6:16–21):
Jesus came to the disciples in their storm. How has Jesus met you in seasons of fear or uncertainty—and how is He calling you to trust Him now?

Healing the Man Born Blind (John 9:1–12):
Spiritual sight is often harder than physical sight. Where might you need to ask Jesus to help you see more clearly—yourself, others, or even Him?

Raising Lazarus (John 11:1–43):
Jesus called Lazarus out of the tomb. What part of your life feels lifeless or stuck—and how might Jesus be calling you to new life, even now?

23

Nicodemus: From Shadows to Light

Nicodemus, a Pharisee and a respected member of the Jewish ruling council, appears three times in the Gospel of John. His story unfolds as a journey from uncertainty and secretive inquiry to a public act of faith, culminating in his involvement in the burial of Jesus.

The first time we encounter Nicodemus, he comes by night to speak with Jesus (John 3:1-21). He approaches Jesus in the darkness, perhaps out of fear of his peers or simply because he needs the quiet of the night to process his thoughts. The conversation with Jesus is one of the most profound in the Gospels, as Jesus speaks of being "born again" and explains the new birth through the Spirit. Yet Nicodemus struggles to grasp the meaning of Jesus' words. He is a learned man, but the idea of spiritual rebirth challenges the foundation of everything he knows.

In this conversation, Jesus reached back into the Jewish Scriptures to draw out the instance of the brazen serpent (Numbers 21). This is a passage with which Nicodemus would be familiar. Jesus stated that just as Moses lifted up the image of the serpent on a pole in the middle of the camp during the plague of serpents during the Exodus, so must the Son of Man be lifted up.

Nicodemus knew the details—anyone bitten would die, but if the turned (an act of faith) and looked at the brazen serpent lifted up on the pole for all to see, they would be healed (saved, restored). No doubt, this was another puzzling comment from Jesus. First talking about being born again; then, talking about the Spirit, and now talking about the Son of Man being lifted up.

Although Nicodemus might have been looking for answers, he was bombarded by confusing images—birth, wind, serpent. He was left with more questions than answers.

In the second instance, during the Feast of Tabernacles (John 7:37-52), Nicodemus appears again, this time defending Jesus subtly within the Sanhedrin. He raises a question about the legality of condemning someone without first hearing them out, a question that makes his fellow Pharisees uncomfortable. This moment suggests that Nicodemus is torn—he sees the truth in Jesus' words but remains cautious, unsure how to fully embrace the message of the Kingdom of God.

Finally, after Jesus' crucifixion, Nicodemus steps fully into the light. He joins Joseph of Arimathea to prepare Jesus' body for burial (John 19:38-42). This act of honor marks a significant shift for Nicodemus. No longer hidden in the shadows, he takes a public stand as a disciple of Jesus along with Joseph of Arimathea, offering spices and linens to wrap Jesus' body. His actions speak louder than words—they reveal a heart transformed by the very message of Jesus, the message he had struggled to understand three years before.

"Lifted Up"

By night, Nicodemus sought the Light,
In shadows deep, a question bright.
"What must I do to see Your face?"
He asked, unsure of Heaven's grace.
"Born again," the Savior spoke,
A new birth from above, a life awoke.
But still he pondered, still he feared,
In night's embrace, the path unclear.
But then came dawn—his heart did know,
The cross revealed what darkness sowed.
As Moses raised the serpent high,
So Christ was lifted up to die.

Through shadows deep, to light he came,
With Joseph bold, he called His name.
No longer hiding, fear aside,
He honored Christ, the crucified.

Analysis:

Nicodemus' journey is one of progression, moving from a place of hiddenness to a place of public faith. Initially, he is drawn to Jesus out of curiosity but remains in the darkness of uncertainty, unable to fully comprehend the radical nature of Jesus' message about the Kingdom of God. The conversation in John 3 is pivotal, it marks a confrontation between Nicodemus' earthly understanding of the law and the spiritual rebirth Jesus offers. Jesus' reference to the serpent lifted up in the wilderness (Numbers 21:4-9) is a foreshadowing of His own death, an act that would bring salvation to all who believe.

In John 7, Nicodemus steps forward slightly, defending Jesus in a way that suggests his internal conflict. He cannot yet fully take a stand, but his defense is a sign that his faith is beginning to grow. His willingness to question the actions of his peers is significant—it shows that the seeds of belief have been planted.

Finally, in John 19, Nicodemus' actions reveal the culmination of his faith journey. His anointing of Jesus' body with burial spices was a courageous and public act of devotion—a bold shift from the man who once came to Jesus by night.

The phrase "lifted up," which Jesus spoke in John 3, takes on deeper meaning. Now grasping the full significance of the cross, Nicodemus steps into the light to honor the crucified Messiah—the One lifted up for the healing of the nations, just as the bronze serpent was lifted in the wilderness to bring salvation to the Israelites.

Nicodemus' journey invites readers to reflect on their own faith journey. Like him, many of us start in the shadows, uncertain and questioning. But as we encounter the truth of Christ, we are called to step into the light—both in belief and action. Nicodemus' story challenges us to examine where we are in our journey of faith, urging us to move from secrecy to openness, from doubt to certainty, and from shadows to the full revelation of Christ's love and sacrifice.

Reflections

1. Nicodemus came to Jesus with questions—but also with hesitation. When have you found yourself seeking Jesus quietly, in the shadows? What held you back?

2. Jesus spoke of being *"born from above"* as the only way to truly see the Kingdom of God. How would you describe your own experience of spiritual rebirth? What changed for you?

3. Nicodemus saw the Son of Man lifted up. How does the image of Jesus on the cross help you understand the Kingdom of God and your place within it?

4. Nicodemus moved from secrecy to courage. Where might God be inviting you to step more fully into the light of faith—publicly, personally, or spiritually?

Notes for your Journal:

24

The Woman at the Well
–Living Water

The encounter between Jesus and the Samaritan woman at Jacob's well (Jn. 4:1-42) marks a pivotal moment in His ministry—a demonstration of His willingness to break social, cultural, and religious barriers to bring the message of salvation to all, especially those deemed outsiders. Samaria was a land that most Jews avoided, due to the deep animosity between Jews and Samaritans. Yet Jesus *must needs go through Samaria* (Jn. 4:4), implying divine necessity.

As Jesus sat by the well, weary from His journey, a woman from the Samaritan town of Sychar arrived in the heat of the day—likely to avoid the other women who came in the cooler morning hours. Her timing spoke of her reputation and the weight of her past. Jesus, in His humanity, was thirsty and tired, yet in that moment, the Father had work for Him to do.

Their conversation began with a simple request for water, but it soon transformed into a profound spiritual dialogue. Jesus offered the woman *"living water,"* a metaphor for the eternal life He alone could provide. Despite her initial confusion, she eventually realized that this was no ordinary man. Jesus spoke what the Father revealed (John 8:26) about her personal history—knowledge only a prophet or the long-awaited Messiah could possess. This moment of revelation led to a radical shift in her understanding of Jesus. She declared, *I know that Messiah is coming. When He comes, He will tell us all things* (Jn. 4:25), to which Jesus replied, *I who speak to you am He* (Jn. 4:26).

Jesus did not simply offer her physical refreshment—He invited her into the fullness of life. Her shame, isolation, and questions were not barriers to Him. She left her water jar behind and ran to share the news with her town. Her testimony became a catalyst for belief. Many in Sychar came to see Jesus for themselves, and they acknowledged Him as "the Savior of the world."

"Living Water"

He walked where none would go,
Through roads that led to hate,
A Jewish man by ancient well,
Whose thirst would open fate.
She came, with heart weighed down,
The midday sun her friend,
A woman lost, but here she'd find
A truth that would not end.
"Give me water," He did ask,
But she, unsure, could not yet grasp
The gift of life He came to bring—
A wellspring rising, Living Spring.
A flood of waters, pure and free.
"Give this living water to me,
That I may never thirst again."
"Living water," He proclaimed—
by grace alone, He washed her shame.
He knew her life, her deepest pain,
Yet still He spoke with grace,
He offered what the world could not—
A love no time could erase.
And she, once lost, now ran to tell
The townsfolk of her King—
The One who knew her every sin,
And gave her life to sing.

The encounter at the well reveals the profound depth of Jesus' mission. The Samaritan woman represents the marginalized, the outcast, the one living in shame—yet Jesus not only acknowledges her but approaches her with an offer of grace that transcends her brokenness. This scene underscores several key themes: the humanity of Jesus, His divine mission, and His revelation as the Messiah.

First, the humanity of Jesus is evident. He is tired, thirsty, and vulnerable, experiencing the physical limitations of human life. Yet in His humanity, He is also divinely commissioned to engage with this woman, who is otherwise invisible in the societal structure. Jesus' weariness gives way to a divine purpose—a reminder that while He shared human frailty, He was under direction of the Father.

Jesus' conversation with the woman is a moment of divine revelation—He spoke what the Father gave Him to say. As He later said, *I do nothing on my own authority, but speak just as the Father taught me* (John 8:28). This was an invitation for her to see the deeper spiritual truth He is offering.

She initially misunderstands about living water, thinking in physical terms. But Jesus slowly leads her from physical thirst to a spiritual understanding of the "living water" He offers, which symbolizes eternal life through the Holy Spirit. This water is not merely for physical refreshment but for the restoration of the soul—a transformation that fulfills the deepest needs of every human heart.

When Jesus reveals Himself as the Messiah (as clearly as He ever revealed Himself), it is a moment of great significance. Unlike His interactions with the Jewish religious leaders, where He often spoke in parables or veiled His identity, He openly declares to this Samaritan woman—an outsider, an individual with a troubled past—He was the Christ. This is a remarkable revelation, highlighting the inclusive nature of Jesus' mission: He came not only for the Jews but for all people, regardless of their past or their status in society.

The woman's response is one of immediate transformation. She leaves behind her water jar, a symbolic gesture of leaving her old life behind, and goes to share the news of Jesus with her community. Her testimony is powerful. It pointed others to the reality of Jesus' identity and the life-changing power He offers. The message of living water is not just for the woman, but for her whole town—illustrating how an encounter with Jesus ripples out to others.

Jesus' interaction with the Samaritan woman powerfully reminds us that He came to offer living water to all—no one is excluded from His grace. His mission was not constrained by religious or social norms; it was a mission to seek and save the lost, to heal the brokenhearted, and to offer eternal life to all who come to Him in faith.

Reflections

1. Jesus met the woman at the well in the midst of her ordinary routine, carrying the weight of her past. When has Jesus met you in an ordinary place and turned it into a sacred moment?

2. The woman came alone, likely due to shame or rejection by others. How do shame or fear of judgment still keep people—especially women—from community or from Jesus? What does her story teach us about how Jesus sees those who feel unseen?

3. Jesus offered *"living water"* to one considered an outsider. What does this teach us about the heart of God? Who are the people today that we might overlook—or who might feel unworthy of grace?

4. After encountering Jesus, she left her water jar and ran to tell others. What would it look like for you to leave something behind and step into boldness? Is there a "jar" you need to put down?

5. Her voice, once silenced by shame, became a catalyst for others to believe. How has your story or testimony impacted others? Where might God be calling you to speak up and share what He's done in your life?

25

The Proclamation of the Kingdom

After the wilderness, Jesus begins His public ministry, proclaiming the arrival of the Kingdom of God. *The time has come*, He declares, *The Kingdom of God has come near. Repent and believe the good news!* (Mark 1:15). This announcement is not a quiet, passive statement—it is a bold declaration that God's reign is now breaking into history through the person of Jesus. (See page 22 as a reminder.)

This is the Kingdom that Jesus will embody and demonstrate through His healings, miracles, and teachings. It is a Kingdom where the lost are found, the sick are healed, and the poor are blessed. But it also requires a radical change of heart. The Kingdom of God demands repentance, turning from sin and self-centeredness, and turning to God's will and way of living.

For the people of Israel, this announcement is a hopeful and challenging message. The Kingdom they had been waiting for is not what they expected—it is not one of political freedom from Rome, but a deeper, spiritual freedom that transcends earthly powers.

"The Kingdom is Near"
"Repent—the Kingdom is near," He cries,
A voice that shakes the heavens and skies.
A Kingdom built on truth and light,
Where wrong is righted, dark made bright.
Not by might, nor by sword will it come,
But through love, through peace, through God's own Son.
A Kingdom not of power, but of the heart,
Where weak are made strong, and the broken take part.
Come, enter this Kingdom, leave all behind,
A new way of living, a new way to find.

Analysis: The Kingdom's Radical Arrival

Jesus' proclamation of the Kingdom marks a new era in God's redemptive plan. It is not a distant hope but a present reality, inaugurated through the life and ministry of Jesus Himself. The Kingdom of God is at hand.

For the Jewish people, this announcement was revolutionary. They had longed for a political Messiah who would deliver them from Roman oppression, but Jesus offers a radically different vision. The Kingdom He proclaims is not of this world. It is a spiritual Kingdom that transforms the hearts and lives of its citizens.

This proclamation calls for a radical reorientation of life. Repentance and belief are the keys to entering this Kingdom. Two words capture the essence of conversion: 1) *metanoia*—to change the mind, to change the direction; 2) *epistrepho*—includes the element of faith—not just turning from something, but also turning to something or someone (Acts 26:19-20). The Kingdom demands a change of heart, a turning away from sin and self-centeredness, and a turning toward God's will.

Reflections

1. Jesus proclaimed that the Kingdom of God had come near. What does it mean to you that God's reign is not only future but already present in the world through Christ?

2. The Kingdom begins with repentance and belief. How do you understand repentance—not just as sorrow for sin, but as a radical reorientation toward God's way of life?

3. Jesus' Kingdom challenged people's expectations. In what ways do your own expectations of how God "should" work need to be reshaped by the reality of His Kingdom?

4. This Kingdom welcomes the broken, the weak, and the humble. How does that vision of the Kingdom give you hope? How might it challenge your assumptions about strength, success, or influence?

26

The Rejected Messiah

In Luke 4:14-30, we find a pivotal moment in the ministry of Jesus that marks the first significant rejection He experienced. After His time in the wilderness and the early stages of His ministry in Judea and Galilee, His fame began to spread. Jesus was recognized for His wisdom and the authority with which He spoke, and many were amazed by His teachings. But the turning point came when He returned to His hometown of Nazareth, where He would face skepticism and rejection from those who knew Him best.

When Jesus entered the synagogue on the Sabbath, He was handed the scroll of the prophet Isaiah. He read from a well-known messianic prophecy, proclaiming that the Anointed One would bring good news to the poor, proclaim liberty to captives, and heal the blind. After reading the passage aloud, He declared boldly, *"Today this Scripture has been fulfilled in your hearing."* He was identifying Himself as the Messiah, the one who would bring liberation, healing, and the year of the Lord's favor.

At first, the crowd was amazed at His words, marveling at the graciousness of His speech. But doubts quickly arose among them. *"Isn't this Joseph's son?"* they asked. They knew Jesus. They had watched Him grow up in their small town, and they could not understand how He could be the fulfillment of such grand prophecies. In their minds, the Messiah was supposed to be a political and military liberator—not a humble carpenter's son from Nazareth.

Jesus, aware of their skepticism, responded with a prophetic challenge. He suggested that they would demand signs from Him, just as He had performed miracles in other towns. He reminded them that no prophet is accepted in his hometown, and He used the examples of Elijah and Elisha, who extended God's grace to Gentiles rather than Israelites, to highlight the broader scope of His mission. This subtle reference to Gentiles ignited the crowd's anger, as they had expected a Messiah to restore the glory of Israel, not extend God's grace beyond its borders.

In their anger, the people of Nazareth tried to throw Jesus off a cliff, but He calmly passed through the crowd and left, continuing His ministry elsewhere. This moment marks the beginning of Jesus' rejection by His own people. It highlights the tension between the messianic expectations of Israel and the reality of the Messiah they encountered. Jesus was not the military leader they envisioned; He was a humble servant, offering peace, healing, and reconciliation in ways they could not yet comprehend.

"The Scroll and the Word"
He stood where they had known Him well,
The boy who learned to read and tell,
Of prophecies that spoke of grace,
But now, a man before their face.
The synagogue, a sacred space,
And He unrolled the ancient scroll,
To read aloud with heart and soul,
Words of the prophet from long ago,
Words that promised peace below:
"The Spirit of the Lord is near,
To heal the blind, to calm the fear,
To set the captive free, proclaim
The year of God's redeeming reign."
He paused, and in that silent beat,
The air around Him felt complete.
"Today," He said, "this word is true,

In Me, the Lord is coming through."
They marveled first—such grace, such light,
But soon the shadows blurred the sight.
"Is this not Joseph's son?" they said.
"How can He be the One they've read?"
Familiar face and carpenter's hands,
Not royal robes, not palace lands.
And so they grumbled, doubts began,
This humble man, this child of man,
Could one so common bring the dawn?
And they rejected Him, withdrawn.
He spoke of prophets far and wide,
Of healing done for those denied—
Of Gentiles saved, and Israelites lost—
A message far too great a cost.
For He was not the One they sought,
The king with armies they had thought,
But in His words, a truth unfurled,
He came to save a broken world.
And in their wrath, they turned to hate,
For love and grace they could not wait.
They pushed Him out with bitter hands,
And sought to end His earthly plans.
But He, undaunted, walked away,
His mission still for another day.
A kingdom built on love and peace,
Where all are welcomed, all find release.

Analysis:
This instance reflects the critical moment when Jesus, returning to
Nazareth, faces rejection from His hometown. Initially, the people of
Nazareth are filled with awe at His words, recognizing the power
and authority in what He says. However, their admiration quickly

turns to skepticism. They see Him as a familiar figure—Joseph's son—and they cannot reconcile His humble background with their expectations of the Messiah.

The turning point in this story is the moment when Jesus declares that He is the fulfillment of the messianic prophecy. This declaration should have been the pinnacle of His revelation, but instead it triggers doubt and anger among the people. The core of their rejection stems from their narrow, nationalistic view of God's kingdom. They expected a Messiah who would bring political liberation and military victory, someone who would restore Israel's power. But Jesus' message was broader and more radical: *He came not just for Israel but for the Gentiles as well.* His reference to Elijah and Elisha healing Gentiles reveals that God's mercy and grace would extend beyond the borders of Israel.

In the synagogue, the people's initial admiration is evident as Jesus reads from Isaiah 61:1-3—one of the great Messianic prophecies. The weight of the words Jesus read from the scroll was evident—familiar to a people awaiting the coming of the Anointed One. Their awe turns quickly to growing doubt and eventual rejection as they struggle to accept that Jesus was applying these words to Himself. He was claiming to be the Anointed One. They knew this man. Who did He think He was? They knew His father. How could the Messiah come from such humble beginnings? Their rejection escalates to violence as they attempt to throw Jesus off a cliff, revealing the deep frustration and disbelief they felt.

This incident illuminates a key aspect of Jesus' mission: He was not a political Messiah but a servant who would bring peace, healing, and salvation to the world. His mission would challenge Israel's exclusive view of God's plan and extend grace and mercy to all people, including Gentiles. Jesus' calm departure from the scene symbolizes His unwavering commitment to His mission—a mission that would eventually lead Him to the cross, where the full scope of God's love and grace would be revealed.

This moment of rejection in Nazareth sets the tone for the growing tension that would accompany Jesus' ministry. Throughout His life, He would continue to defy the expectations of those around Him, challenging their understanding of God's Kingdom and ultimately revealing a radical new vision of God's love and salvation for the world.

Reflections

1. The people of Nazareth marveled—then turned to rejection. Why do you think it was so hard for them to accept that someone they *knew* could be the fulfillment of God's promise? Have you ever struggled to see God at work in familiar places or people?

2. Jesus' message challenged national pride and religious assumptions. What expectations or assumptions about God's work in the world might you need to lay down in order to fully embrace His Kingdom?

3. The crowd was offended that grace extended beyond Israel. How do you respond to the idea that God's mercy is sometimes given to those you wouldn't expect or even agree with? What does that reveal about the wideness of God's love?

4. Jesus walked away from their rejection. What might His calm departure teach us about responding when we are misunderstood, dismissed, or rejected for our faith?

Journaling: Halfway with the Messiah

You've now traveled through half of this journey, watching the Kingdom of God unfold in surprising and often unsettling ways. This moment—the rejection at Nazareth—invites a pause. Take some time to write, reflect, and pray through what this book has stirred in you so far. There is no "right" way to reflect here. Let the Spirit guide you. What matters most is to pause, listen, and respond.

What have you noticed about the way Jesus interacts with people—
especially the unexpected ones?

Have any moments in these stories felt especially personal? Which
ones, and why?

How is your understanding of the Kingdom of God shifting? What is
God's Spirit showing you?

Is there any place in your life where you are resisting what Jesus is
doing—because it feels too familiar, too unexpected, or too different
from what you thought faith would look like?

Write a prayer of response. Thank Jesus for revealing Himself in
fresh ways. Confess anything He has gently brought into the light.
Ask for courage to walk in step with His Kingdom—even when it
defies your expectations.

When you're ready, continue this journey walking with Jesus, who
still chooses the road of grace, even when crowds turn away.

27

The Authority of the Kingdom

In Luke 4:31-44, we find a critical period in Jesus' ministry as He begins His public work in earnest. After the rejection in Nazareth, Jesus settles in Capernaum, a bustling town on the northern shore of the Sea of Galilee, which becomes the hub of His early ministry. This moment marks the transition from the initial, more private phase of His mission to a public declaration of His authority. It sets the tone for how He will engage both physical and spiritual realms.

Jesus' teaching in the synagogue on the Sabbath is met with astonishment. His words possessed authority that was unlike anything the people had ever heard before. He didn't merely expound on existing scripture—He spoke with the direct authority of the One who authored it. As He taught, a man possessed by an unclean spirit cried out, revealing an uncanny recognition of Jesus' veiled divine identity: "*I know who you are—the Holy One of God.*" The demonic spirit saw what others could not. In this encounter, Jesus demonstrates His power over physical afflictions and also over spiritual forces. Rebuking the demon, it leaves the man without harm.

The crowd is amazed at His authority, but there is more to Jesus' work. He doesn't just cast out demons—He heals the sick, as evidenced by the healing of Simon Peter's mother-in-law from a high fever. This miracle is followed by a torrent of healings as people bring their sick and demon-possessed to Jesus, and He cures them all. Interestingly, while the demons recognized Him as "*the Son of God,*" Jesus silenced them, unwilling to allow even the demons to proclaim His true identity at this stage of His ministry.

After a night of healing and teaching, the following morning,

Jesus retreats to a desolate place for solitude and prayer. The people, desperate for His continued presence and miracles, search for Him, pleading with Him to stay. However, Jesus responds with a mission statement that will define His ministry: *I must preach the good news of the kingdom of God to the other towns as well; for I was sent for this purpose.* Even though the crowds sought Him, Jesus knew His mission was far broader than the immediate needs of those gathered in Capernaum. He was to spread the message of the Kingdom of God, and that message could not be confined to one place.

This moment in Capernaum marks the beginning of a broader movement. It highlights the growing recognition of Jesus' divine power and authority—among His followers and in spiritual realms. It establishes the importance of His preaching ministry, which transcended mere healing and miracles. Jesus was laying the foundation for the revelation of God's Kingdom. While His miracles confirmed His authority, His message was one of far greater significance.

"The Holy One of God"

He spoke in words they'd never known,
With power, with weight, with sovereign tone,
The scroll of God in His hand unfurled,
And every word reshaped their world.
In Capernaum, beneath the sun,
The crowds began to gather, stunned.
"Who is this man who speaks with grace,
Whose very words the dark displace?"
Then from the shadows came a cry,
A voice that pierced the stillness high—
"Ha! What do You want with us today?
Have You come to drive us all away?"
The demon trembled in its hold,
And yet, it knew the truth, so bold,
"I know You—You are the One,

The Holy One, God's own Son!"
But with a word, He spoke and stilled
The trembling spirit, bent and filled
With darkness. "Be silent, come out," He said,
And peace descended, as the demon fled.
The crowd was left in awe and fear,
"What is this word that we now hear?
With power and might, He casts them down,
These demons flee, and yet He's crowned."
But more was yet to come that night,
The sick were healed and wrong made right.
A fever broke at His command,
Touched by grace, they made their stand.
The demons screamed, "You are the One,"
But He rebuked them, silence done.
His time had not yet come, you see,
The Kingdom of God would set them free.
But when the dawn had broken through,
He slipped away from those who knew
Only the healer, not the name—
The One who'd set their hearts aflame.
He went to pray, to seek the will,
Of God the Father, calm and still.
But when they came, He said with care,
"I must go, the Kingdom declare.
The good news waits in other lands,
For this is why my Father stands
To send me out, to speak, to heal,
To show the world His Kingdom's Seal."
And so He moved, with power to bring,
The Kingdom's joy, the Kingdom's King.
The crowds may gather, and demons cry,
But God's great purpose will not die.

We see both the awe and the tension of these early moments in Jesus' ministry. The people are astonished by His authoritative teaching, but the demons' recognition of Jesus as *"the Holy One of God"* reveals a deeper, more profound understanding of His role and identity than the people themselves could grasp. Their fear and recognition of Jesus' power serve as a stark contrast to the crowd's wonderment, signaling the cosmic weight of His mission.

Jesus' silencing of the demons is emphasized in the poem as a deliberate choice, underscoring that while the recognition of His power was important, the timing and manner of His revelation were crucial. His identity as the Messiah could not be defined by demonic forces but had to be revealed in the fullness of time. This moment of silence highlights the tension between Jesus' divine mission and the people's desire for immediate, miraculous signs.

The healing miracles and their significance point to the broader purpose of Jesus' ministry: the Kingdom of God. While healing and exorcisms were important signs of His power and authority, they were always secondary to the message He came to proclaim—the good news of the Kingdom of God.

Finally, Jesus' withdrawal to a desolate place for prayer and His refusal to stay in Capernaum underscore the divine purpose that shaped His mission. Though the people wanted Him to stay and perform more miracles, Jesus knew His calling was to proclaim the Kingdom beyond Capernaum. This moment sets the tone for His itinerant ministry and shows that while the miracles were vital, they were not the end in themselves—they were signs pointing to the greater reality of God's Kingdom (Matthew 12:28).

Reflection:

The people sought miracles, but Jesus moved on to proclaim the Kingdom elsewhere. Are there places in your life where you want God to stay and "do more"—but He's inviting you instead to trust His broader purpose?

28

Kingdom of Freedom
The Sabbath Controversies

The issue of the Sabbath controversies plays a critical role in understanding the tension between Jesus and the Jewish religious leadership, particularly the Pharisees. Jesus' interactions with them, especially on matters of the Sabbath, were not just about observing a day of rest. At a deeper level, these controversies became a battleground for Jesus to reveal the nature of the Kingdom He came to establish. For the Pharisees, the Sabbath was a symbol of their rigid understanding of righteousness—an outward observance that, in their view, separated the righteous from the unrighteous. A litmus test.

In contrast, Jesus' understanding of the Kingdom of God was radically different. The Kingdom was not about adhering to a list of rules and regulations but about heart transformation. Jesus did not come to abolish the Law but to fulfill it—fulfilling the Law meant that its deepest purpose could now be experienced relationally with God through Jesus Himself. The Kingdom that Jesus proclaimed was about reconciliation, healing, and the liberation of individuals—expressed through faith, grace, and compassion rather than legalism.

The Pharisees' legalism was rooted in an understanding of righteousness based on external conformity. They saw righteousness as something that could be earned by following rules, and they believed they had exclusive access to it through their diligent adherence to the Law. Jesus, however, showed them that true righteousness is not earned by following external rules but by being transformed from the inside out. When Jesus healed the paralyzed man in Mark 2:1-12, He demonstrated that forgiveness and healing were the true marks of the Kingdom of God, not rule-keeping.

The Sabbath controversies, especially in Mark 2:23-3:6, illustrate the stark contrast between Jesus' understanding of the Kingdom and the Pharisees' approach. Jesus' healing of the man with the withered hand on the Sabbath was not an act of defiance against the Law but an illustration of the Kingdom's heart: mercy over sacrifice, healing over ritual, people over regulations. Jesus was not dismissing the Law, He was fulfilling its ultimate purpose—to bring people into a life-giving relationship with God.

The Pharisees' constant accusations and criticisms were rooted in their misunderstanding of Jesus' mission. They were focused on external conformity and missed the very heart of God's Kingdom—which is about restoration, freedom, and grace. This misalignment with the true message of the Kingdom, built on love and compassion, eventually led to the Pharisees' rejection of Jesus and His eventual death on the cross. This conflict led to a collusion between the Herodians and the Pharisees—traditional enemies. They wanted to kill Jesus (Mark 3:6). The controversies and cross are connected.

The Kingdom of God that Jesus preached was not a kingdom of rules, but of relationship. It was a Kingdom where freedom from the law, not slavery to it, defined true righteousness. The Kingdom was about entering into a new covenant with God, where faith, trust, and an intimate relationship with God were the foundational markers. Jesus came to reveal that relationship with God through Him was the only way to truly enter the Kingdom (John 1:12-13).

"The Kingdom of Freedom"
The Pharisees stood, their rules in hand,
Guardians of the law, a strict command.
With rigid hearts and eyes of stone,
They searched for sins that none had known.
They saw the Sabbath, cold and still,
A day of rest, by human will.
They thought the Kingdom, made of law,

Would bind us tight, no release or flaw.
But Jesus came, the Kingdom new,
A Kingdom built on grace, not rule.
He touched the sick, He healed the blind,
He broke the law to free the mind.
The man whose hand was withered, drawn
He healed on Sabbath, love had shown.
"Is it wrong to heal, to give release?
God's Kingdom comes, not to oppress,
But to bring life, to set you free,
To see the heart, not what you see."
No chains to bind, no lists to check,
A life transformed, a love unchecked.
The Kingdom is not made of stone,
But of hearts restored, and grace alone.
So Jesus calls, to all who hear,
Come, follow Me, be free from fear.
The rules are gone, the chains removed,
Enter the Kingdom, be redeemed, renewed.

Analysis:

What we're seeing in these Sabbath controversies is a fundamental misunderstanding of the Kingdom of God—an issue that not only confronted the Pharisees in Jesus' day but continues to be relevant today. The Kingdom that Jesus came to reveal was not about conformity to rules and regulations but about entering into relationship with God through Him. This is the radical message Jesus preached, and it turned the expectations of the people upside down.

The Pharisees' attempt to build a righteousness based on external compliance mirrors what many people still believe about religion and spirituality. People are often taught religion is about following rules—whether the rules are the commandments of a religious tradition, moral codes, or social standards. But Jesus constantly confronted this worldview, revealing righteousness in the Kingdom of God is not about rule-keeping but about heart transformation through grace.

When Jesus healed on the Sabbath or broke the rules, He was not rejecting the law; He was fulfilling its true purpose—to restore and heal humanity. This is why He could say that He had come not to abolish the Law, but to fulfill it (Matt. 5:17-20). He was showing that the Kingdom of God, rather than being a kingdom of rules, was a kingdom of freedom—freedom from the law's power, freedom to love, to heal, to forgive, and to live in relationship with God.

These Sabbath confrontations and the tension with the Pharisees were significant markers in the growing conflict that would lead to the cross. The Pharisees' misunderstanding of the Kingdom of God—as one of external legalism—was in direct contrast to Jesus' mission to bring about a new relationship with God, not through works or rule-keeping, but through faith in Him as the Messiah.

The Kingdom of God is a kingdom of paradox: the religiously devout may be far from it, while the broken, the outcast, and the humble are often the first to recognize its arrival. This stark contrast would define Jesus' entire ministry and would eventually lead Him to the cross, where He would complete His mission: to offer freedom and grace to those who are willing to lay down their own self-righteousness and embrace the new Kingdom He came to reveal.

This is why understanding the Sabbath controversies is so crucial—not just for understanding the dynamics between Jesus and the Pharisees but for grasping the deeper truths about the Kingdom of God that Jesus introduced. This is a Kingdom of grace over law, mercy over sacrifice, and relationship over ritual—a Kingdom that begins in the hearts of those who trust in Jesus and extends to the world as a message of hope and freedom.

Reflection:

What does it look like for you to live in the freedom of God's Kingdom—where love, grace, and relationship matter more than rules, expectations, or appearances?

29

The Call to a Higher Righteousness

Jesus stood before a vast crowd on a mountainside, a place where He often found solitude to pray and commune with His Father. This time, however, He was surrounded by people eager to hear His words. Among them were the multitudes who had followed Him from villages far and wide, hoping for healing or to witness miracles. But there were also the scribes and Pharisees, those self-proclaimed keepers of the law, who scrutinized Jesus' every word, hoping to find fault.

As the crowds gathered, Jesus began to teach, addressing the very heart of what it meant to belong to the Kingdom of God. *"Blessed are the poor in spirit, for theirs is the kingdom of heaven,"* He said. These were words not just for the destitute or the oppressed, but for anyone who recognized their utter dependence on God. With each beatitude, Jesus revealed a Kingdom that was not about power or prestige but about humility, mercy, and purity of heart. He described the heart that reflected God's own—one that thirsted for righteousness, that was pure, that mourned sin, and that was willing to make peace.

But then, Jesus went further. He made a striking declaration: *Unless your righteousness exceeds that of the scribes and Pharisees, you will never enter the kingdom of heaven.* This statement sent a shockwave through the crowd. One could almost hear the gasp. To the common people, the scribes and Pharisees were the gold standard of righteousness. They were the ones who kept the law meticulously, who fasted, who tithed—who seemed to live out the very essence of what it meant to be righteous.

But Jesus was saying that the righteousness of the Kingdom wasn't outward conformity to the law—it wasn't mere rule following. No, the righteousness He was talking about was deeper, more transformative. It was a righteousness of the heart that transcended actions and rituals. He would go on to say, *"You have heard that it was said, 'You shall not murder,' but I tell you that anyone who is angry with their brother is guilty of murder in his heart."* The Kingdom of God was not about external rituals or conformity to law. It was about the transformation of the heart—love, mercy, forgiveness, and purity.

He was not abolishing the law, but fulfilling it. The law pointed to the heart of God. Jesus called His followers to reflect that heart.

"The Kingdom Heart"

A kingdom not of gold or throne,
But of the heart, where love is sown.
Blessed are the poor, the meek, the low,
For in this heart, God's rule shall grow.
The law was written, line by line,
But love transcends, and mercy shines.
Not in the keeping of the rule,
But in the heart when grace breaks through.
To those who mourn, to those who seek,
To those who hunger, the lost, the weak,
The Kingdom's call is clear and loud—
The humble heart, not a hardened crowd.
Righteousness, not for show or gain,
But pure in heart, through joy and pain.
The law of love, the law of grace,
Transformed within, our hearts embrace.

Analysis: The Righteousness of the Kingdom

In the Sermon on the Mount, Jesus challenges the prevailing religious norms of His time. The Pharisees and scribes had reduced the complex law of God to a set of rules and regulations—rules that could be obeyed outwardly while the heart remained unchanged. They built a system where outward conformity became the measure of righteousness, where following the rules earned God's favor.

But Jesus' proclamation was revolutionary. True righteousness, He taught, isn't just about what we do outwardly—it's about who we are inwardly. It's about a heart that seeks God, that reflects His love and mercy, and that lives in harmony with His will. This is a righteousness that exceeds the law—because it reaches deeper than behavior and touches the very core of who we are as people.

The "righteousness" Jesus speaks of here is the righteousness that He Himself embodies. It is fueled by love, mercy, and humility, not pride, power, or self-righteousness. The Pharisees and scribes were more concerned with ritual purity and maintaining the appearance of holiness than with genuine love for God and people. Jesus, however, called His followers to a Kingdom heart—a heart that was pure, that sought reconciliation, that forgave the unforgivable, and that was willing to serve and love others without condition.

This is the essence of the Kingdom of God that Jesus came to reveal: a Kingdom not of external obedience, but of internal transformation. It's not about keeping the letter of the law but living in the spirit of the law, loving God and loving people. The standard for Kingdom citizens—a heart loving deeply and serving humbly.

For those listening to Jesus, it must have been both a shock and a comfort. Shock, because the bar was set so high—righteousness was no longer a matter of outward performance, but of internal transformation. Comfort, because the Kingdom was not about achieving perfection through ritual or law-keeping—it was about having a heart that was open to God's grace, that could receive forgiveness, and that could extend forgiveness to others.

Connecting to the Kingdom: A New Righteousness

This teaching of Jesus brings us back to our central theme: the Kingdom of God is unlike any kingdom the world knows. It's not a kingdom of political power, wealth, or military might. It's a kingdom of the heart, a kingdom where love reigns, where mercy is abundant, and where the greatest among us are those who serve.

The righteousness of the Kingdom is a gift—one that cannot be earned through rule-keeping but must be received through faith. This was the contrast Jesus sought to expose with the Pharisees: their righteousness was based on outward conformity to the law, but the righteousness of God, which Jesus offered, could only be received through grace, faith, and transformation.

As we reflect on Jesus' call for a righteousness that exceeds that of the scribes and Pharisees, we must remember that the Kingdom of God is not about achieving personal holiness through effort—it's about receiving God's grace and living in response to it. This is the heart of the good news that Jesus came to bring. The Kingdom of God is not a distant, unreachable goal; it is something that is accessible to all who are willing to humble themselves and seek God's transformative power.

Jesus' declaration of the Kingdom's ethics and standards gives us a profound insight into how we should live as citizens of that Kingdom. It also sets the tone for the rest of Jesus' ministry—emphasizing that the Kingdom of God isn't just about laws to follow; it's about a relationship with God that transforms the heart and spills out into every aspect of our lives.

Reflections

1. Jesus calls us to a righteousness of the heart. Where do you see the difference between outward rule-keeping and inward transformation in your own walk with God?

2. The Beatitudes paint a portrait of the Kingdom heart. Which one speaks most deeply to your present spiritual hunger—and why?

3. Jesus said our righteousness must exceed that of the Pharisees. What does that look like in practical, everyday faith?

30

The Debtor

In Luke 7—the woman anointing Jesus' feet at the house of Simon
the Pharisee—powerfully contrasts the Kingdom values that Jesus
came to reveal and the self-righteousness of the Pharisees. It exposes
the difference between religious ritual and true repentance, between
rigid law-keeping and gracious forgiveness. The way the Pharisees
responded to the woman and the way Jesus responded to her reveals
two completely different approaches to the Kingdom of God and to
the nature of grace.

The evening was still, but the hearts of those gathered in Simon's
house were far from it. Simon, a Pharisee—devout, respected—
invited Jesus to dinner, perhaps out of curiosity, perhaps to test Him.
The meal began, and the conversation flowed, but the air was thick
with judgment.

A woman, known by all to be a sinner, heard that Jesus was at
the Pharisee's house. She came in, uninvited, but driven by something more profound than simple curiosity. She approached Jesus
from behind, weeping. Her tears fell freely onto His feet, and she
wiped them with her hair, kissing them and anointing them with precious ointment.

The room grew silent, then murmured with disapproval. "If this
man were truly a prophet," Simon thought to himself, "He would
know who this woman is. He would never allow her to touch Him."
But Jesus knew Simon's heart. He turned to him and said, "*Simon, I
have something to say to you.*"

Simon, a man of law and order, nodded. "Say it, Teacher."

Jesus spoke of a moneylender with two debtors: one owed five hundred denarii, the other fifty. Both were unable to pay, but the moneylender canceled their debts. Jesus asked, "Which of them will love him more?"

Simon, reluctant but willing, answered, "The one who was forgiven more."

"*You have judged rightly*," Jesus replied, turning toward the woman, but speaking to Simon. "*You see this woman? You did not wash my feet, but she has washed them with her tears. You did not greet me with a kiss, but she has not stopped kissing my feet. You did not anoint my head with oil, but she has anointed my feet with ointment.*"

And then came the stunning conclusion: "*Her sins, which are many, are forgiven—for she loved much. But he who is forgiven little, loves little.*"

Turning to the woman, Jesus said, "*Your sins are forgiven.*" The guests at the table muttered among themselves, "*Who is this, who even forgives sins?*"

And Jesus spoke directly to the woman: "*Your faith has saved you; go in peace.*"

"The Feet of Mercy"

In Simon's house, the table was set,
But hearts were hardened, eyes were wet,
A woman known by all to sin,
Came quietly, trembling, to begin.
She stood behind with tears in flow,
Wiping His feet, her love to show.
Her hair let down, her hands so bold,
Anointed feet with oil of gold.
The Pharisee, in judgment's gaze,
Rebuked her actions, as out of place.
"Does He not see what she has done?

A sinner's touch—can He be the One?"
But Jesus, knowing hearts so true,
Told Simon what he never knew:
"For those forgiven much, they love,
And mercy flows from God above."
He turned to her with tender grace,
"Your sins are gone, you found your place.
Your faith has saved you, peace is near,
Go forth now free, my daughter dear."
And in that room where whispers fell,
Jesus' love, a sacred spell,
Revealed the Kingdom in the dust—
A place for those who love, and trust.

Analysis:

This story is a beautiful picture of the Gospel in action, but it also
serves as a sharp critique of the Pharisees' approach to righteousness
and grace. Simon, the Pharisee, embodied everything the religious
elite valued: adherence to the Law, strict social boundaries, and self-
righteousness. He invited Jesus into his house, but his heart remained closed off. He performed the expected rituals, but without a
deep understanding of grace. His response to Jesus and the woman
showed a lack of humility—a refusal to see his own need for forgiveness and transformation.

In contrast, the woman—a sinner, a social outcast—knew the
depth of her sin and her need for mercy. Her actions of washing Jesus' feet, wiping them with her hair, and anointing them with oil
were acts of extravagant love and devotion. They were a visible expression of her faith, a faith born of the understanding that God's
mercy was available to her, no matter her past. Her tears and her actions were signs of repentance—but they were also acts of faith, an
expression of her love for the one who could forgive and heal.

The parable Jesus tells is key here. The two debtors, one owing more than the other, represent two types of people: those who understand the magnitude of their debt (their sin) and those who do not. The woman recognized the great debt she owed and, thus, the great mercy she had received. Simon, on the other hand, thought he had little to be forgiven for—and so, his love remained shallow and his worship incomplete.

Jesus' point is clear: true worship, true love, and true forgiveness come from a humble recognition of our need for grace. Simon's failure to offer Jesus the expected hospitality (washing feet, kissing, anointing) was a reflection of his spiritual pride. He saw no need for grace because he believed he was already righteous. Meanwhile, the woman, despite her reputation, understood that grace was her only hope—and she loved much because she was forgiven much.

This incident highlights the Kingdom values that Jesus came to reveal:

- *Priority of the Kingdom of God*: Jesus consistently pointed to relationship with God over ritual or religious observance. His words to Simon—*"her sins, which are many, are forgiven—for she loved much"*—show that true righteousness is about heartfelt faith, not outward compliance.

- *Priority of People Over Things*: Jesus was not concerned with the social status of the woman or her past. His priority was her heart, her faith, and her need for grace. This stands in stark contrast to Simon's judgmental attitude, which measured a person's worth based on their reputation or adherence to societal standards.

- *Priority of Servanthood*: The woman's act of humble service—washing Jesus' feet with her tears and anointing Him with ointment—embodies the servant-hearted love that Jesus advocated for. Jesus, who came to serve, saw this act as beautiful worship. Meanwhile, Simon, with his legalistic and prideful heart, missed the heart of the Kingdom altogether.

The forgiveness Jesus offers in this scene points to the nature of His Kingdom: it is a place of grace, freedom, and transformation. Everyone, regardless of their past, is invited into this Kingdom. The path is through faith and repentance, and the result is a heart that loves deeply because it has been forgiven greatly.

This moment in Luke 7 is a powerful illustration of the contrast between Jesus' Kingdom and the legalism and self-righteousness that so often stands in opposition to it. The woman, a sinner, entered Simon's house to offer worship, and Jesus not only received her offering but also affirmed it as the highest expression of love and devotion. Meanwhile, Simon's cold, ritualistic observance of the Law prevented him from entering into the true worship of the Kingdom of God.

The Kingdom of God is not about the outward signs of ritual or the accumulation of knowledge. It's about relationship, grace, and love—the kind of love that leads to deep, humble service and radical forgiveness. This is the Kingdom Jesus revealed, and this is the Kingdom we are called to embrace.

Reflections

1. Jesus said, *"He who is forgiven little, loves little."* How has your experience of God's forgiveness shaped the way you love and worship Him?

2. Simon's judgment of the woman revealed his own blind spots. Are there people or situations you tend to judge before seeing their heart?

3. The woman's tears, touch, and gift were all acts of love. How do you express your love and gratitude to Jesus for His mercy?

4. Jesus saw what Simon could not—the woman's faith. How does this story challenge your understanding of worship, humility, and who belongs in the Kingdom?

Journaling: A Heart That Loves Much

This moment—intimate, awkward, redemptive—invites reflection from the heart. In the space that follows, write your own response to Jesus, just as the woman did, not with words spoken aloud, but with tears, gratitude, and honesty.

Write about a time you felt the weight of your own "debt"—a moment of failure, shame, or sorrow. What did grace look like then?

How does it feel to know that Jesus sees your heart and welcomes your worship, even when others might not?

Where have you been like Simon—slow to extend grace or blind to your own need for forgiveness?

What might extravagant love look like in your life right now? What act of worship, service, or devotion might reflect your gratitude?

A Prayer of the Forgiven:

Use this space to write your own prayer—a prayer of thanks, confession, or renewed surrender. You might begin with:
Jesus, You see me as I am—and You welcome me still. You know my sins, yet You offer peace. I have been the debtor, and You have paid what I could never repay...

31

A Clash of Expectations

We often approach the ministry of Jesus in small segments—a sermon here, a Bible study lesson there, a few verses in our daily devotionals or readings. But when we fail to look at the larger picture, we miss the profound arc of His mission. Let us zoom out and examine a key segment of His ministry captured in Matthew 10-12, where we gain valuable insights into both Jesus' actions and the expectations of those around Him.

To set the stage, we should first establish a timeline for the ministry of Jesus, one that helps us contextualize these events. Here is an outline of the time frame for the three-year public ministry.

- Early Judean Ministry: 6 months
- Galilean Ministry: 18 months
- Period of Withdrawals: 6 months
- Later Judean Ministry: 3 months
- Perean Ministry: 3 months
- Last Week and Resurrection Appearances

This gives us a general time frame of three years for the ministry of Jesus. While scholars sometimes debate whether the ministry lasted three years or three and a half, we'll focus on the three-year framework for our purposes.

In understanding Jesus' ministry, we see it unfold in three major movements, each of which reflects a distinct strategy:

1. **Launching the Ministry** – In this first phase, Jesus ministers alone. It's a "one-man show," where He sets the course for what is to come.

2. **Calling the Twelve** – As the need for broader engagement grows, Jesus calls the Twelve Apostles and sends them on a preaching tour, expanding His influence across the region. In essence, He's "taking the band on the road"—to maintain our music analogy.

3. **Refining the Twelve** – Finally, Jesus invests in the ongoing training of His Apostles, preparing them to lead in His absence—what we might metaphorically call "cutting the album" as they lay the foundations for the future of the movement.

Matthew's gospel provides key hinge points that help us see these transitions. One of the first summaries of Jesus' ministry appears at the end of chapter 4:23:

"And he went throughout all Galilee, teaching in their synagogues and proclaiming the gospel of the kingdom and healing every disease and every affliction among the people."

This brief statement encapsulates the early period of Jesus' ministry—His introduction to the people of Galilee through His teaching, preaching, and healing.

We then encounter a second summary in Matthew 9:35-38. By this time, Jesus' ministry has grown, and the crowds are becoming larger and more desperate for His attention. Matthew writes:

"And Jesus went throughout all the cities and villages, teaching in their synagogues and proclaiming the gospel of the kingdom and healing every disease and every affliction."

But Matthew adds something new this time: *When he saw the crowds, he had compassion for them, because they were harassed and helpless, like sheep without a shepherd. Then He said to His disciples, "The harvest is plentiful, but the workers are few. Ask the Lord of the harvest, therefore, to send out workers into His harvest.*

In this moment, we see a significant shift. Jesus recognizes the growing need for others to take on the responsibility of ministry. A plentiful harvest demands more laborers. Jesus tells His disciples to pray for workers to be sent into the harvest, signaling the transition from His solo ministry to a team-oriented one.

The Appointment of the Twelve: A New Phase

After a night of prayer, Jesus calls twelve of His disciples, appointing them as Apostles (Matthew 10:1-4). These twelve were not just followers; they were now commissioned (*apostolos* = one sent with a commission) to carry on His work. What Jesus had been doing on His own—teaching, healing, casting out demons—He now entrusted to them, empowering them to act in His name.

Matthew 10 provides the detailed instructions for their mission. Jesus tells them to proclaim that the Kingdom of God is at hand (10:7). But He also gives them the authority to perform signs and wonders—healing the sick, cleansing lepers, raising the dead, and casting out demons (10:8). This commission signals a direct engagement in spiritual warfare. The Twelve are now the hands and feet of Jesus in the world, confronting the powers of darkness and ushering in the reign of God.

The Clash of Expectations

But as the Twelve take on this mission, they are not the only ones struggling with expectations. Jesus, too, finds Himself caught in a whirlwind of conflicting hopes and beliefs about the kind of Messiah He was supposed to be.

In the early days of His ministry, the people longed for a political Messiah—a ruler who would restore Israel's greatness and deliver them from Roman oppression. They hoped for a king who would wield power and authority—perhaps even militarily—bringing judgment on Israel's enemies and a just reign to the land. But as Jesus began His ministry, healing the sick, casting out demons, and proclaiming the Kingdom of God, it became clear that He was not the Messiah they had anticipated. Instead of acting as a conquering king, Jesus demonstrated the reality of a spiritual kingdom—one rooted not in political revolution, but in healing, mercy, and repentance.

This tension came into sharp focus when John the Baptist, the one who had paved the way for the Messiah, found himself in prison. John had expected the Messiah to bring swift judgment and liberation. But Jesus' ministry was different, marked by compassion and mercy rather than wrath and political upheaval. In a moment of doubt, John sent his disciples to ask Jesus, *Are you the One who is to come, or should we expect someone else?* (Matthew 11:3). Jesus responded by pointing to His works: the blind see, the lame walk, the dead are raised. These were the signs of the Kingdom—but not the signs of a political warrior.

Meanwhile, the Pharisees—the religious authorities who upheld the law—watched Jesus with increasing suspicion. They expected a law-abiding leader who would restore Israel's spiritual purity by enforcing the law. But Jesus was not afraid to break their rigid rules. He healed on the Sabbath, a direct challenge to their interpretation of the law, and when He cast out demons, the Pharisees accused Him of being in league with Satan.

In response, Jesus declared, *If it is by the Spirit of God that I cast out demons, then the Kingdom of God has come upon you* (Matthew 12:28). This was a bold declaration: every miracle Jesus performed was evidence that the Kingdom of God had arrived, but not in the way they had envisioned. The Kingdom was not one of political power or military might—it was a spiritual reign, one that entered the hearts of individuals who submitted to God's will.

The Pharisees, still demanding a sign, were told that the only sign they would receive was the sign of Jonah—the sign of Jesus' death, burial, and resurrection. His rejection of their request for signs was yet another subversion of their expectations.

In a poignant moment of redefining His true "family," Jesus also redefined the nature of the Kingdom. His mother and brothers came to visit Him, but He was surrounded by a crowd. When told they were outside, Jesus pointed to those around Him, saying, *Whoever does the will of My Father in heaven is My brother and sister and mother* (Matthew 12:50). Here, Jesus emphasized that His Kingdom was not about physical family ties or political affiliations—it was about spiritual obedience to God's will.

"Kingdom Unseen"

They waited for a king with sword in hand,
To heal the broken faith and cleanse the land.
A mighty warrior, in battle array,
To drive the Romans far away.
But the Kingdom came, not with a crown,
But in humble grace, breaking powers down.
Through healing hands, through mercy's touch,
A reign of love that asked for trust.
John from prison asked, "Is this the One?
Or shall we wait for another to come?"
But Jesus' answer echoed clear,
A Kingdom of healing, not of fear.
The Pharisees asked for a sign,
To prove He was the King divine.
But Jesus, firm, would not yield,
The sign of Jonah—the only reveal.
Then His family came to see,
But Jesus showed them plainly:
The ones who do the Father's plan,
Are family to Him, woman, man.
A Kingdom not by power or might,
A reign of grace that shatters night.
A Kingdom of mercy, of love's decree,
A reign within, where hearts are free.

Analysis: The Kingdom Subverted

Jesus' ministry throughout the Gospel of Matthew confronts the deeply entrenched expectations of His time regarding the Messiah.

155

For the Jewish people, the Messiah was meant to be a political savior—a military leader who would overthrow their oppressors and re-establish the throne of David. This vision was shaped by centuries of longing for national liberation and justice.

However, Jesus consistently subverted these expectations by redefining the nature of the Kingdom of God. The Kingdom, as He proclaimed it, was not about political dominance or territorial restoration—it was about the reign of God in the hearts of individuals.

The signs He performed—healing the sick, casting out demons, forgiving sins—were evidence of a different kind of Kingdom, one that broke into the world through spiritual transformation and divine mercy rather than through force or political might.

John the Baptist, the forerunner of the Messiah, struggled with this redefinition. His expectations were deeply shaped by the hope for a messianic figure who would bring judgment and establish God's justice on earth. Jesus' actions of healing and mercy, while fulfilling Old Testament prophecy, did not fit the mold John had envisioned. This created a tension, reflected in John's question, *Are you the One, or should we expect someone else?*

The Pharisees, too, had their own expectations. As religious authorities, they hoped for a Messiah who would uphold the law and restore purity to Israel through strict observance of the Torah. Jesus' disregard for their traditions—such as healing on the Sabbath—was seen as blasphemous. Their demand for signs further illustrated their misunderstanding: they wanted Jesus to prove Himself through miraculous displays of power, expecting the Messiah to come as a warrior king who would meet their expectations.

In contrast, Jesus' response to their request for signs was both direct and profound: He refused to accommodate their desires. The *"sign of Jonah"* pointed to the deeper reality of His mission—His death, burial, and resurrection—which would ultimately demonstrate His identity as the true Messiah (Romans 1:4).

Finally, Jesus' teaching about family in Matthew 12:50 further subverted societal expectations. In a culture where family ties were paramount, Jesus redefined true kinship not by blood but by spiritual obedience. Those who did the will of God were His true family. This radical redefinition underscored the nature of the Kingdom: it was not about ethnic identity, physical lineage, or political allegiance. It was about spiritual allegiance to God and His will.

The Kingdom of God, as Jesus taught, was a rule that begins in the hearts of individuals who choose to yield to God's reign. It is a Kingdom of grace and mercy, not one of political power or conquest. This was a radical departure from the expectations of the Jewish people, including John the Baptist, the Pharisees, and even His own family. And it is this subversion of expectations that defines the nature of Jesus' mission and the Kingdom He came to establish.

Reflections

1. John asked, *"Are you the One?"* Have you ever questioned God's timing or direction because He didn't meet your expectations? What was the outcome of that waiting?

2. Jesus empowered the Twelve and sent them out. Where might Jesus be calling you to step out of your comfort zone and join in His Kingdom work?

3. The Pharisees demanded signs—but missed the Kingdom in front of them. Are there places in your life where you're looking for proof, instead of trusting God's presence?

4. Jesus redefined "family" as those who do the will of God. How does this challenge your sense of belonging, responsibility, or connection to the Body of Christ?

Journaling: Kingdom in Conflict

This vignette brings us into a moment of growing tension—between expectation and reality, between religious control and radical mercy. Jesus didn't come to conform to our hopes but to reshape them. In the space that follows, reflect honestly on the clash between your expectations and God's Kingdom.

Where have you struggled with Jesus not being the kind of Savior you expected?

Are there areas in your life or ministry where you're sensing resistance—not from enemies, but from misunderstandings or misplaced hopes?

What does it look like for you to participate in a Kingdom that is seen through healing, mercy, and service, not power or applause?

When have you felt called to something that others didn't understand or affirm? How did you respond?

A Prayer for Alignment

Use this space to write your own prayer. Ask God to align your heart with His Kingdom—not as you expect it to be, but as He reveals it. You might begin: *Jesus, I confess how often I come to You with my own agenda—my idea of what Your Kingdom should look like. But You are not here to serve my plans. You are here to rescue, restore, and reign in ways I don't always understand...*

32

The Kingdom in a Touch

Every healing was an expression of the Kingdom of God. These were signs that the Kingdom of God had come in power. Remember what we just stated: In Matthew 12:28, when Jesus is accused of casting out demons by the power of Beelzebul, His response is crucial. He links the casting out of demons with the arrival of the Kingdom of God—because the exorcism is not simply about freeing a person from a demon but about the disarming of the powers of darkness and the establishment of God's sovereign rule.

In the midst of His public ministry, the demand on Jesus' time and energy became overwhelming. Crowds followed Him everywhere, seeking healing, teaching, and miracles. The sheer number of people and the weight of their needs created a constant strain on His spirit. The miracle of healing the leper, in particular, was not just a demonstration of divine power but also a moment that illustrated the deep emotional and physical cost of His ministry.

Luke details the incident: *While he was in one of the cities, there came a man full of leprosy. And when he saw Jesus, he fell on his face and begged him, "Lord, if you will, you can make me clean." And Jesus stretched out his hand and touched him, saying, "I will; be clean." And immediately the leprosy left him. And he charged him to tell no one, but "go and show yourself to the priest, and make an offering for your cleansing, as Moses commanded, for a proof to them." But now even more the report about him went abroad, and great crowds gathered to hear him and to be healed of their infirmities. But he would withdraw to desolate places and pray* (Luke 5:12-16).

The leper, covered in a disease that separated him from society, had the courage to approach Jesus. He begged, *Lord, if you will, you can make me clean*. His words were an expression of faith but also an acknowledgment of the power and authority Jesus carried. When Jesus reached out, touching the man, He broke a societal and religious taboo—the touch of a leper was seen as contaminating. Yet, in that act, Jesus didn't just heal the man; He embraced his pain, his alienation, and his need for wholeness. In that moment, the leper was not only healed—he was restored to wholeness and reconnected with God's love.

As the word spread about Jesus' miracles, the crowds grew larger and more desperate. People sought healing for their physical ailments, but many also wanted a glimpse of the Kingdom He was preaching. Yet, Jesus knew that in the midst of the demand, He needed to retreat. The power to heal, to teach, to perform signs was not His—it was through the Father's will and the Spirit's power that He worked. In His human existence, Jesus was a conduit for the work of God.

Though fully divine, Jesus, in His earthly ministry, chose to live in total dependence upon the Father. His humanity—vulnerable, tired, emotionally taxed—was not shielded from the demands of His mission. This profound mystery of the God-man is central to understanding how He operated: always in communion with the Father and always directed by the Spirit, even in His most trying moments.

As the *Logos*, when He made the decision to become a man, He surrendered the prerogatives of His divinity. John 1:1 and 1:14 affirm this mystery. And the early hymn quoted by Paul explicitly states that the *Logos* made the decision Himself to lay aside the privileges and prerogatives of His attributes and took upon Himself the intrinsic attribute of a man—a servant man—who would become a dead man (Philippians 2:6-11). Jesus, in His humanity, was totally dependent upon the power of the Spirit and the Father to work through Him (Mt. 12:28; John 5:19, and 14:10).

An important healing event occurred that gives insight into how God's power worked through Jesus. It is recorded in Mark's gospel. Here are the details: *And when Jesus had crossed again in the boat to the other side, a great crowd gathered about him, and he was beside the sea. Then came one of the rulers of the synagogue, Jairus by name, and seeing him, he fell at his feet and implored him earnestly, saying, My little daughter is at the point of death. Come and lay your hands on her, so that she may be made well and live. And he went with him.*

On the way, *a great crowd followed him and thronged about him. And there was a woman who had had a discharge of blood for twelve years, and who had suffered much under many physicians, and had spent all that she had, and was no better but rather grew worse. She had heard the reports about Jesus and came up behind him in the crowd and touched his garment. For she said, "If I touch even his garments, I will be made well." And immediately the flow of blood dried up, and she felt in her body that she was healed of her disease. And Jesus, perceiving in himself that power had gone out from him, immediately turned about in the crowd and said, "Who touched my garments?" And his disciples said to him, "You see the crowd pressing around you, and yet you say, 'Who touched me?'"*

And he looked around to see who had done it. But the woman, knowing what had happened to her, came in fear and trembling and fell down before him and told him the whole truth. And he said to her, Daughter, your faith has made you well; go in peace, and be healed of your disease (Mark 5:21-34).

When the woman touched His garment, she knew something had happened in her body. She knew she had been made whole. But Jesus also knew that someone had touched Him in faith and had drawn off power from Him. He sensed it.

When He stopped the throng and asked who touched Him, His disciples motioned to the crowd and said essentially, "What do you mean who touched you? Everyone is touching you."

Jesus searched the crowd, locked eyes with the woman...and He knew who touched Him. She just wanted to melt into the crowd. But Jesus blessed her and said that her faith had made her well.

Jesus sensed that power had left Him. Like a vessel being poured out, He was a living channel of divine power. It flowed from Him and through Him. And when that power is depleted, it had to be replenished. Jesus withdrew to desolate places to pray, to reconnect with the source of His strength—His relationship with the Father.

The retreat was not merely a withdrawal from the crowds—it was an intentional re-centering of His heart on the Father. Without this continual replenishment, even Jesus, in His humanity, would have been overwhelmed by the constant demands of His ministry. In this retreat, Jesus aligned Himself with the Father's will, receiving not just strength, but also the sustaining peace needed to continue His work.

In a world full of noise and demands, the Kingdom of God is not just about action; it is about restoration. The rhythms of the Kingdom require retreat, prayer, and solitude to truly be able to serve and fulfill the role each person has in the Kingdom's unfolding. Jesus, the conduit of God's Kingdom, shows us that even in our busiest moments, we must make time to withdraw, to reconnect with God, and to be replenished for the journey ahead.

"The Touch and the Retreat"
A leper knelt with trembling hands,
His body scarred, his strength undone.
With faith he whispered, "If you will,
You have the power—make me clean."
A touch—so simple, yet profound—
A healing touch that knew no bound.
The skin restored, the heart made whole,
In that moment, God touched his soul.
But crowds grew loud, needs pressed near,

A kingdom sought, their hopes sincere.
The healings flowed, the teachings clear,
But Jesus knew—He must disappear.
For even He, the Son of Man,
Without retreat, could not sustain.
He turned aside to fill the well,
Hear the Father's call, in Him to dwell.
Power that flows, through hands that give,
Must first be filled for us to live.
In stillness, silence, we renew,
The Kingdom grows in hearts made new.
So Jesus, knowing what it takes,
Retreat to prayer His path to make.
To serve, to heal, to teach, to show,
He needed rest, He needed flow.
And so must we, in work and strife,
To serve the Kingdom, in our life—
In silence, prayer, our hearts restored,
To serve and heal, by God's accord.

Analysis:

This passage and the accompanying poem bring to light the importance of spiritual restoration in the life of anyone engaged in the work of God's Kingdom. The leper's healing is a powerful sign not just of Jesus' compassion and divine authority but of the deep connection between faith and wholeness. But alongside the miracles is the truth that even Jesus needed time to withdraw and be restored in prayer. The idea that miracles and service are not just one-time acts of power but require ongoing renewal resonates deeply in the context of the Kingdom. Jesus demonstrates that the Kingdom is not about constant action but about balance—the need for rest, the need to be replenished by God, and the call to serve out of that refilled spiritual well.

Just as Jesus was the conduit of the Father's power, we, too, are called to be conduits of God's love and strength, but that requires time in solitude and prayer to ensure that we are functioning not from our own strength but from God's. This speaks to the Kingdom's rhythm—action and retreat, giving and receiving, working in harmony to fulfill God's purposes. The Kingdom Jesus revealed was not one driven by constant activity, but shaped by a holy rhythm—balancing action with quiet, service with silence—a Kingdom that is as much about the unseen retreat as it is about the public healing.

Reflections

1. When the leper said, *"If you will, you can make me clean,"* he demonstrated both faith and humility. How does your own prayer life reflect trust in God's will, even when you are in need?

2. Jesus touched the untouchable, breaking societal and religious barriers. Are there people or situations you tend to avoid, even though Jesus might call you to engage with compassion?

3. The woman with the issue of blood believed that even touching Jesus' garment could heal her. What does her bold faith stir in you? In what area of your life are you reaching out for healing?

4. Jesus sensed that power had gone out from Him and later withdrew to pray. What does this teach you about the rhythm of giving and receiving in your own walk with God?

5. The pattern of Jesus' ministry included retreat for restoration. How might you create space for silence, solitude, and spiritual renewal in your own life?

33

Feeding the 5,000
A Crisis of Expectations

The feeding of the 5,000 stands as one of the most remarkable and pivotal moments in the ministry of Jesus. Recorded in all four Gospels, it marks the pinnacle of His popularity and sets the stage for a profound shift in His ministry. With only five loaves of bread and two fish, Jesus miraculously fed a multitude—5,000 men, plus women and children (John 6:9)—demonstrating both His compassion for the crowd and His reliance on the Father's power at work through Him. Yet, as we explore this event, we also see how the miracle exposed the deep-seated messianic expectations that surrounded Him.

The crowd's reaction to the miracle was swift and intense. They recognized something extraordinary had happened, and in that moment, they identified Jesus as *"the Prophet"*—the one promised by Moses, who would deliver them from their current oppression (John 6:14). They wanted to make Him king by force (John 6:15), hoping He would become the political and military leader they envisioned, the one who would liberate Israel from Roman rule and provide for their material needs.

However, Jesus, fully aware of their motives, compelled the Apostles into a boat and go to the other side of the sea. He dismissed the crowd. Then, He withdrew into a mountain to pray. The intent of the crowd to take Him by force and install him as king was a very real temptation. If He wanted to be an earthly king, this was the best chance. But this was not the kind of kingship He had come to offer. His mission was not to meet their immediate, earthly desires, and be a temporal ruler. His mission was to reveal a far deeper, spiritual reality—the Kingdom of God breaking into the world.

The Crisis of Expectations

The next day, the crowd followed Him across the Sea of Galilee, eager to see more signs and experience more of His miraculous power. But Jesus confronted them with a stark challenge. *You are looking for me, not because you saw the signs I performed, but because you ate the loaves and had your fill* (John 6:26). Here, Jesus made it clear that the crowd's fascination with Him was superficial.

They sought Him for the bread that filled their stomachs, not for the spiritual nourishment He offered for their souls. In a moment of teaching that shocked them, He declared, *I am the bread of life* (John 6:35). He went further, stating that unless they ate His flesh, drank His blood, they had no part in Him (John 6:53). This was profound, difficult teaching, one that the crowd found impossible to accept.

The challenge was too great. Unable or unwilling to understand, they turned away in confusion and offense. The promise of earthly bread was what they wanted; the invitation to partake in the deeper, sacrificial meaning of His life was too much for them to bear. Jesus, in the face of this rejection, turned to His disciples, asking, *You do not want to leave too, do you?* (John 6:67).

This was not just a test of loyalty; it was a moment of revelation for both Jesus and His followers. The rejection of the crowds marked a critical turning point in Jesus' ministry. He would no longer allow the desire for a political Messiah to be layered upon Him. His Kingdom was not about worldly power, but about a spiritual revolution that required a radically different mindset.

Peter, in a moment of clarity, responded on behalf of the twelve, *Lord, to whom shall we go? You have the words of eternal life* (John 6:68). Though they did not fully understand the mystery of Jesus' words, they recognized that He was the one who held the key to eternal life. This declaration was both a confession of faith and an acknowledgment of the deep truth found in Jesus alone. Despite the doubts, the twelve stayed, choosing to remain with Him even as many of the crowd walked away.

The Aftermath: A New Phase of Ministry

The aftermath of the feeding of the 5,000 and the subsequent fallout with the crowds set the stage for the next phase of Jesus' ministry. This moment marked the end of the second year of His public ministry and the beginning of what would come to be known as the "Period of Withdrawals." Several key events precipitated this shift:

- **The Return of the Twelve**: Jesus' disciples had just returned from their preaching tour, and their report likely reinforced the need to prepare them for the deeper lessons ahead. The crowds that had once clamored for His miracles were no longer an asset but a distraction from the mission at hand.

- **John the Baptist's Death**: The tragic death of John the Baptist at the hands of Herod was a dark reminder of the dangers Jesus faced. It also made it clear that the political authorities were beginning to see Jesus as a threat. Jesus, aware of the risks, withdrew further from public ministry.

- **The Turning of the Crowd**: With many abandoning Him over His radical teachings, Jesus faced a crisis of expectations. The popular sentiment that had once fueled His ministry was now shifting, and He had to decide whether to appease the masses or stay true to His divine calling. Jesus chose to focus on the few who truly understood, the twelve disciples who would carry forward His mission after His death.

"He Is the One"
The Miracle of Bread

Five loaves, two fish—plenty to begin,
Thousands were hungry, their energy thin.
He blessed, He broke, He gave the bread,
And all were filled, their hunger fed.
But the bread He gave was not just for the day—

The Kingdom was coming in a whole new way.
Not crowns or thrones or swords to wield,
But grace revealed in a broken field.

The Bitter Turning
"Eat of My flesh, drink of this cup,"
The feast of the soul, heaven lifts up.
But hearts grew hard, confusion spread,
They could not grasp the words He said.
"This teaching's hard, how can it be?"
They longed for freedom, not mystery.
They came for signs, for power and throne,
Not for a Savior who stood alone.
And many turned and walked away,
Their hopes too small to truly stay.

Will You Also Go?
Then Jesus turned, His voice grown low,
"Will you leave too?"—they had to know.
But Peter spoke with faith held fast,
"To whom shall we go? Only Your words last.
We believe You are the Holy One—
The Christ, the Lord, God's True Son."
They stayed, though confused, with questions still,
Held not by answers—but by committed will.

Analysis:
The feeding of the 5,000 is a moment that encapsulates the tension at the heart of Jesus' ministry: the clash between human expectations and the true nature of God's Kingdom. The crowds wanted a king who would fulfill their immediate, material needs. But Jesus' Kingdom was never about fulfilling physical desires; it was about addressing the deeper spiritual hunger that lies within every human heart. By rejecting the crown the people wanted to give Him and calling them to something deeper, Jesus demonstrated that His mission was not to meet temporal needs but to offer eternal life.

This moment also highlights the personal crisis faced by Jesus' followers. The temptation to conform to popular expectations and the pull of immediate gratification were real challenges. But the disciples, led by Peter, made a decisive choice to remain with Jesus, recognizing that the truth of eternal life was found in Him, even when it did not align with their earthly hopes or understanding.

The shift to the Period of Withdrawals was not a retreat in defeat but a necessary step in preparing for the final phase of Jesus' mission. It was a time of deeper teaching and preparation for His closest followers, a moment to lay the foundation for the radical nature of the Kingdom He would establish.

In the end, the feeding of the 5,000 was a sign, a miraculous display of Jesus' divine authority, but it was also a message that challenged the crowd's understanding of what the Messiah was meant to be. The miracle pointed beyond the loaves and fish to a much deeper truth: that Jesus Himself is the Bread of Life, the one who satisfies the soul's deepest hunger. And the question He posed to His disciples remains just as relevant today: *"Will you also leave?"*

Reflections

1. Have you ever felt drawn toward success, recognition, comfort—knowing the Spirit was calling you to surrender or a harder path?
2. When have you been disappointed by unmet expectations—asking for one kind of provision, and being offered something deeper and more difficult to accept.
3. Can you recall a time when you had to leave a "crowd" or a place of momentum—because the Spirit was compelling you to move on for your own growth?

Journaling: A Crisis of Expectations

At the height of His popularity, Jesus was tempted—not by weakness, but by opportunity. The crowd wanted to make Him king by force. The disciples may have felt the pull too. Mark tells us Jesus *compelled* them into the boat—urgent, deliberate (Mark 6:45-46). Was it to protect them? Or to keep them from joining in?

Jesus knew that kingship without the cross was not the way of the Kingdom.

What expectations—yours or others'—have you needed to walk away from?

What voices in your life need silencing so you can hear the Father's?

Use this moment to consider honestly your expectations. Let it be a time of realignment. You might close with a prayer like this:

Jesus, sometimes I want You to be something You are not. I confess the ways I try to shape You to meet my needs or fit my comfort. Teach me to want what You give, and to follow You—whether or not the crowd understands. (How would you continue?)

One person responded like this:
"Jesus, sometimes I want You to be something You are not.
I confess the ways I try to shape You to meet my needs or fit my comfort.
Teach me to want what You give,
and to follow You—whether or not the crowd understands.
When You offer bread I don't understand,
help me not to walk away.
When You call me to solitude or surrender,
give me the courage of Peter to say,
"To whom else shall I go?
Speak truth to the deep hunger within me—
and let Your words become my life."

34

The Crisis of Commitment

After the feeding of the 5,000 and the teaching that followed, many of the crowd turned away in confusion and offense. The radical nature of Jesus' words—*"Unless you eat the flesh of the Son of Man and drink His blood, you have no life in you"* (John 6:53)—proved too much for them to bear. It was here that Jesus faced a moment of crisis in His ministry. With so many leaving, He turned to His disciples and asked, *"You do not want to leave too, do you?"* (John 6:67).

This was a pivotal moment, a turning point in Jesus' ministry. The crowd who had followed Him for miracles—and for free food—now rejected Him when He refused to meet their expectations. Jesus was not the political Messiah they had hoped for. This was the peak of Jesus' popularity. The fickle crowd turned their backs on Him.

What had been building for two years, came to a critical moment. The crowd wanted to make Him a king. In their desire, Jesus heard the echo of Satan's temptation to be an earthly king. Dismissing the disciples and the crowd, Jesus went apart to pray, wrestling through this moment in the presence and power of the Father.

This crisis ushered in what would be known as the Period of Withdrawals, a time when Jesus withdrew from public ministry and focused more on teaching His disciples about the nature of the Kingdom. His question to the twelve was not just about their loyalty, but about their willingness to embrace the radical nature of God's Kingdom, even when it defied human logic and understanding.

Peter, in a moment of clarity, responded, *"Lord, to whom shall we go? You have the words of eternal life"* (John 6:68). The twelve, though confused and unsure of all that Jesus had said, were willing to stay, recognizing the truth that was found in Him, even if they couldn't fully grasp it at that moment.

"To Whom Else Can We Go?"

They came for bread—the loaves, the fish,
For signs and wonders, every wish.
But when He spoke of truer Bread,
Of flesh and blood—their spirits fled.
"Eat My flesh, drink My blood," He said—
Doubts rushed in, like floodwaters spread.
Some turned away—their hearts grown low,
But twelve remained—"Lord, where would we go?"
A Kingdom not of earthly fame,
But Spirit-born, in Jesus' name.

Analysis:

The crisis of commitment faced by Jesus and His disciples reveals what it means to follow Jesus. It is not about meeting our earthly desires or fulfilling our immediate wants. The Kingdom of God is about a deeper, transformative relationship with God through Christ, one that challenges our comfort and our expectations.

Peter's response highlights that true life is found in Christ, even when the path is not clear. This moment of crisis, marked by a massive falling away, also marks a key moment in Jesus' mission—He would no longer be able to rely on large crowds but would instead focus on preparing His disciples for the reality of the Kingdom.

Reflections

1. Have you ever experienced a moment when following Jesus meant staying—even when others walked away or when His way didn't make sense? What helped you stay?
2. Peter said, "*Lord, to whom shall we go?*" How would you complete that sentence from your own experience: "*Lord, to whom shall I go? You alone...*"

35

Confession at Caesarea Philippi
Crisis of Perception and Crossroads of Faith

In the region of Caesarea Philippi, amidst the rolling hills and springs of the ancient city, Jesus asked His disciples a question that would ring through the corridors of history: *Who do people say the Son of Man is?* (Matthew 16:13). The disciples responded with varied opinions—some said He was John the Baptist, others believed Him to be Elijah, or perhaps one of the ancient prophets returned.

But Jesus, never content with vague answers, pressed further: *But who do you say that I am?* (Matthew 16:15). This was no idle question—it was an invitation into the heart of the disciples' faith, a moment of profound revelation.

It was Simon Peter who spoke, his words coming not from human insight but from divine revelation: *You are the Christ, the Son of the living God* (Matthew 16:16). This was the moment of confession, where the identity of Jesus as the Messiah was acknowledged openly for the first time by His followers. Yet, despite this breakthrough in understanding, the disciples, including Peter, were still grappling with the nature of the Messiah and His mission.

Their expectations were rooted in a vision of the Messiah as a political and military leader, one who would deliver Israel from Roman oppression. But Jesus, knowing the direction in which His mission was headed, began to tell them that He must go to Jerusalem, suffer at the hands of the religious authorities, die, and rise again on the third day (Matthew 16:21).

Peter, unable to reconcile this vision with his own hopes for a triumphant Messiah, took Jesus aside and rebuked Him. Jesus, in turn, rebuked Peter sharply, saying, *Get behind me, Satan!* (Matthew 16:23). This harsh confrontation revealed the depth of their misunderstanding: though Peter had confessed Jesus as the Christ, neither he nor the others could yet grasp the true nature of the Kingdom—a Kingdom not built through military conquest, but established through the sacrifice of the cross.

"The Question at the Crossroads"

Amidst the rocks where waters churn,
Jesus asked, His voice was firm,
"Who do the people say I am?"
Some spoke of prophets, others of kings,
The answer sought was for deeper things.
Then Jesus asked, with eyes that see,
"And you? Who do you say I be?"
The silence hung, thick with weight,
A question to change each soul's fate.
Peter spoke, bold and clear,
"You are the Christ, the Son so dear!"
The air was still, the rest held their breath,
For in this moment, all life faced death.
But Jesus spoke of the road to the cross,
A kingdom of glory born from loss.
Not through triumph, nor by the sword,
But through suffering and through the Lord.

Analysis:

The conversation at Caesarea Philippi marked another turning point in Jesus' ministry, highlighting the gap between His disciples' expectations and the reality of His mission. Jesus had asked, *Who do you say that I am?* This question went beyond mere intellectual understanding; it called for a personal response that cut to the heart of their faith. Peter's confession—*You are the Christ, the Son of the living God*—was a moment of divine revelation, and yet, even as

Peter declared Jesus' messianic identity, the disciples' perception of what that Messiah would do remained fundamentally flawed.

In this moment, Jesus not only affirmed Peter's confession but also set the stage for His coming Passion. The Kingdom Jesus was inaugurating was not one of military might or political power, but one of suffering, sacrifice, and redemption. It was a Kingdom that would be brought into being through His death on the cross, a truth the disciples struggled to understand.

Peter's refusal to accept this path for Jesus, and Jesus' sharp rebuke, underscored the tension between the human desire for a victorious Messiah and the divine reality of a suffering Savior.

This moment also points to a deeper truth—the Kingdom of God operates on a completely different logic than human kingdoms. The Kingdom Jesus proclaimed was one where the first would be last, where the greatest would be the servant, and where love would be poured out through self-sacrifice rather than dominance.

Peter's confession was the foundation upon which the church would be built (Matthew 16:18), but it would take the unfolding of Jesus' suffering and resurrection for the full depth of this confession to be understood. Even as Jesus' followers came to understand His identity as the Messiah, they would soon realize that the path He walked was not the path they had imagined.

The crisis of perception that began in Caesarea Philippi would only intensify in the weeks to come. As the crowd who once followed Jesus turned away, unable to accept His radical teachings, the disciples would be faced with their own crisis of commitment. Yet, like Peter, they would come to understand that Jesus was not merely the fulfillment of their political hopes but the Savior who would die for the world's salvation.

Ultimately, this moment at Caesarea Philippi lays the foundation for the church's mission, built on the confession of Jesus as the Christ, but also rooted in the cross—a place where victory and defeat, life and death, would be forever intertwined.

Reflections

1. Jesus began by asking, *"Who do people say I am?"*—but quickly turned the question personal. How would you answer today: *"Who do you say I am?"*

2. Peter's confession was bold and true, yet his next words revealed how little he understood the cross. When have you felt certain in faith—but struggled to accept the path God was leading you down?

3. Jesus rebuked Peter not because he lacked faith, but because he resisted sacrifice. Where might you be tempted to follow a triumphant Christ but resist a suffering one?

4. Peter's confession that Jesus was the Christ, the Son of the Living God became the foundation of the church. It is the confession that all followers of Jesus make. But that foundation would only be complete after the cross and resurrection. In what ways is your faith still being shaped by what you haven't yet understood?

36

The Transfiguration

The Transfiguration, occurring just days after Peter's confession at Caesarea Philippi, stands as both confirmation and correction. Peter had boldly declared that Jesus was the Messiah—the Son of the living God—the first open acknowledgment of Jesus' true identity by His disciples. Yet even this moment of divine revelation came laced with human misunderstanding. Peter still imagined a triumphant Messiah, one who would reign without suffering. The disciples saw clearly *who* Jesus was, but not *how* He would fulfill His mission.

To address this, Jesus takes Peter, James, and John to a high mountain, away from the crowds. There, before their astonished eyes, He is transfigured—His face shining like the sun, His clothes becoming dazzling white (Matthew 17:1–2). In this brief but powerful moment, the veil of His humanity is lifted, and His divine glory shines through (the only instance of this in His earthly life). Moses and Elijah appear beside Him, symbolizing the Law and the Prophets—the foundational pillars of Israel's faith—affirming that Jesus is the long -awaited fulfillment of both.

This moment not only affirms the truth Peter had confessed, but it reframes what that truth means. Jesus' Messiahship is not rooted in earthly power or political conquest—it transcends those categories. He is the radiant Son of God, but also the suffering servant foretold in Isaiah 53. The voice from heaven declares, *"This is my beloved Son, with whom I am well pleased; listen to Him"* (Matthew 17:5), echoing the words spoken at His baptism. It is a divine affirmation—but also a divine redirection. The disciples must listen—not just to who Jesus is, but to the kind of Messiah He came to be.

The Transfiguration serves as a brief but profound glimpse into the true nature of Jesus, revealing a divine glory that would remain hidden until after His resurrection. Yet, even in this moment of visible splendor, Jesus remains committed to His earthly mission. He tells the disciples to keep what they have seen a secret, pointing them towards the ultimate revelation that will come with His death, resurrection, and ascension.

"Glimpse of Glory"

On mountaintop, the veil pulled back,
A glimpse of glory now unpacked
Not flesh alone, as men had seen,
But glowing bright in light serene.
Moses stood, and Elijah too,
The Law and Prophets, old and true,
And with the Christ, they spoke of death—
The path to life, to heaven's breath.
The voice of God, a thundered call,
"This is My Son, the Christ of all,"
The moment brief, but clear and bright,
Revealing Jesus' true delight.
Not in the crown, not in the sword,
But in the cross, the Lamb adored.
A kingdom built on love and loss,
To lift the broken, bear the cross.

Analysis: The Theological Significance

The Transfiguration reveals a paradox at the heart of Jesus' identity: He is fully divine, but His divine glory is veiled in His humanity. While on earth, He chooses to live as a servant, humbling Himself to experience the full depth of human life, and only in this rare moment does His true divine nature shine through. It is a glimpse of glory.

This self-limitation—choosing to veil His divine glory and live as a servant—is essential to understanding the nature of the Incarnation. As Philippians 2:5-11 teaches, Jesus did not "empty" Himself by giving up His divinity, but by setting aside the privileges and prerogatives of His divine position, choosing instead to live a fully human life, dependent on the Father.

The appearance of Moses and Elijah emphasizes that Jesus is not only the fulfillment of the Law and the Prophets, but also the completion of their trajectories. Moses, the giver of the Law, and Elijah, the great prophet, both point forward to a Messiah who would fulfill their roles, but also transcend them in a new and surprising way. The voice from heaven, declaring Jesus as God's beloved Son, confirms that Jesus' mission, while fulfilling the law and prophecy, will also involve a suffering and a death that defies the expectations of earthly power.

The Transfiguration not only points to the eternal glory of Jesus but also serves as a pivotal moment in His earthly ministry. It is a foretaste of the glory that will be revealed at His resurrection, yet it also foreshadows the suffering He must endure. The disciples, though amazed, must understand that this moment of divine radiance is but a brief glimpse into the larger story of the Messiah who must suffer, die, and rise again to bring salvation.

The narrative of the Transfiguration, alongside the voice from heaven and the presence of Moses and Elijah, illustrates the truth that Jesus is the fulfillment of God's plan for humanity—one that includes suffering and glory, sacrifice and triumph. As the disciples move forward, they are called to hold this vision of Jesus' glory in tension with the reality of His path to the cross.

Reflections
1. The Transfiguration follows Peter's confession—a moment of clarity followed by confusion. Have you ever had a spiritual high

point followed quickly by a reality check or a difficult truth?

2. God's voice says, *"Listen to Him."* Where do you sense the Spirit nudging you to *really listen* to Jesus—especially in areas where His words might challenge your assumptions?

3. Moses and Elijah represent the Law and the Prophets. In what ways do you see Jesus fulfilling Scripture in your own life— bringing meaning to old truths through new experiences?

4. Jesus told the disciples to keep silent about what they saw until after the resurrection. Why might God sometimes ask us to hold things in silence rather than speak them too soon?

Journaling: Glimpse of Glory, Path of the Cross

The mountaintop was dazzling. But the path ahead still led to Jerusalem. The disciples had seen glory—but they did not yet understand suffering. The Transfiguration asks us to hold both together: divine light and earthly darkness, radiant promise and looming cost.

Reflect on a time when you glimpsed God's glory—through worship, a moment of answered prayer, beauty, or clarity. How did that experience strengthen or challenge your faith?

Where are you now being asked to walk the harder path?

What does it look like to hold onto glory *in the shadow of the cross*?

You might end your journaling with a prayer:
Jesus, I have seen glimpses of Your glory—bright and undeniable. But help me follow You down the mountain too. Teach me...

37

The Way of Greatness

Throughout His ministry, Jesus continually defied the world's expectations, especially in relation to power and greatness. The world's view of greatness is often built upon hierarchical structures, dominance, and control. In this view, those who rise to the top of the pyramid are considered great, while those at the bottom are seen as insignificant. Greatness is about power, authority, and being served by others.

This stark contrast to worldly views of greatness is clearly illustrated in several key moments, particularly in the request made by James and John in Matthew 20:20-28. The two disciples, often referred to as the "sons of thunder," approached Jesus with a bold request: *"Grant that one of us may sit at Your right hand and the other at Your left in Your glory"* (Matthew 20:21). In asking for positions of honor in Jesus' kingdom, they revealed their misunderstanding of the true nature of Jesus' mission. They expected a political and militaristic Messiah, one who would overthrow their oppressors and establish a glorious earthly kingdom where positions of power and influence would be the ultimate goals.

Jesus, however, responded with a rebuke that turned their thinking upside down. He asked, *Can you drink the cup I am going to drink?* (Matthew 20:22), signaling that His glory would come through suffering, not triumph over enemies in the way they envisioned. He then elaborated on the nature of greatness in God's kingdom, saying, *Whoever wants to become great among you must be your servant, and whoever wants to be first must be your slave* (Matthew 20:26-27). Jesus' response redefined greatness entirely—

true greatness is not found in domination or status, but in humble service to others.

This lesson is reinforced in His actions at the Last Supper. As the disciples gathered for the Passover meal, none of them took on the role of the servant to wash the others' feet. In the cultural context, foot washing was a menial task reserved for the lowest of servants. As they entered the room, the basin was prepared. A towel was there. But no servant was stationed to wash their feet. Jesus had told them that greatness in the Kingdom of God was defined by service. Yet, in this upper room, they were still arguing about who was greater and where they would sit (Luke 22:24). None of them took on the role of the servant.

Jesus waited, but no one moved. Not one of them stooped to serve his fellow disciples. Yet, Jesus, their Master and Lord, arose from the table, took a towel and a basin, and washed each of their feet (John 13:1-17). This act of humility shocked the disciples and left them astonished, for they still did not understand the radical nature of His kingdom.

Jesus made it clear: *I have set you an example that you should do as I have done for you* (John 13:15). In this way, He not only taught them the way of greatness, but embodied it Himself.

For Jesus, greatness was not measured by position or power, but by a willingness to serve, to humble oneself, and to give one's life for others. His life was the ultimate demonstration of servant leadership—He did not come to be served, but to serve (Mark 10:45). Jesus called His disciples—and calls us still—to a radically different way of living, one where greatness is defined by self-sacrificial love and service, not by the accumulation of power or prestige.

"The Inverted Kingdom"
They sought to sit on thrones of might,
To grasp at glory, hold it tight,
But in their hearts, the seeds of pride

Were nurtured by the world outside.
They asked to stand beside the King,
In places where worldly power rings,
But Jesus knew the path ahead—
The cross to bear, the road to tread.
He spoke of greatness, not of rule,
But humble hearts, the wise and true.
The greatest in His kingdom's call
Would bend the knee, and serve them all.
With basin low, and towel in hand,
He washed their feet, a humble stand—
The Lord, the Master, set the pace,
To lead by love, to serve with grace.
No thrones were claimed, no glory sought,
The King of Kings, with humble thought,
Revealed the path, the road to rise—
Through death, through love, through sacrifice.
And still today, His words remain,
A challenge to this world's disdain.
The way of greatness, clear and bright—
Is found in service, not in might.

Analysis:

The contrast between the world's view of greatness and Jesus' teachings on greatness is at the heart of His kingdom message. In a society where greatness is often equated with power, authority, and domination, Jesus redefined what it means to be great. His teachings and actions challenge the deeply ingrained human desire for status, recognition, and control. Rather than seeking to climb to the top of a hierarchical pyramid, Jesus invites His followers into an inverted kingdom where true greatness is found at the bottom, in selfless service to others.

In the request of James and John, we see the disciples' struggle to grasp the nature of the kingdom Jesus was establishing. They, like many of their contemporaries, expected the Messiah to bring a kingdom of power, prestige, and political dominance. But Jesus corrected their misunderstanding by emphasizing that greatness in His kingdom is not about seeking positions of power, but about choosing to serve. His words and actions—such as washing the disciples' feet—served as a powerful visual example of this truth. The Son of God, the King of the universe, took on the lowly role of a servant, modeling the true path to greatness.

This radical concept of greatness challenges both the social and spiritual norms of every age. For Jesus, greatness is not about personal achievement or the exercise of power; it is about humility, sacrifice, and serving others. By taking the role of a servant, Jesus showed that the greatest in God's kingdom are those who give themselves for the sake of others, as He Himself would give His life as a ransom for many (Mark 10:45).

For those who follow Jesus, the call is clear: we are to emulate His example of servant leadership. Our measure of greatness is not in how many people serve us, but in how many people we serve. This is the path to true greatness, and it stands in stark contrast to the world's values. In the upside-down kingdom of God, greatness is defined by humility, and true leadership is found in serving others, just as Jesus did.

Reflections

1. Jesus said, *"Whoever wants to become great among you must be your servant."* In what ways does this challenge your own definition of success or significance?

2. Picture the basin and the towel in the upper room. Where in your life is Jesus inviting you to serve with humility—even when no one else steps forward?

38

Was Blind But Now I See

In John 9, we encounter the profound healing of a man born blind, an event that stands in stark contrast to the popular expectations of the Messiah during Jesus' time. The healing itself is a miraculous sign of God's power, but it also serves as a revelation of Jesus' radical departure from the political and militaristic notions of the Messiah that were prevalent in His day.

When Jesus and His disciples encountered the blind man, the disciples asked, *Rabbi, who sinned, this man or his parents, that he was born blind?* (John 9:2). This question reflected the common Jewish belief that suffering was directly linked to sin, either personal or ancestral. However, Jesus' response revealed a different perspective: *Neither this man nor his parents sinned... but this happened so that the works of God might be displayed in him* (John 9:3). In this simple yet profound answer, Jesus redirects the understanding of suffering, not as a punishment for sin but as an opportunity for God's glory to be revealed.

Jesus then performs the healing in a way that defies conventional expectations. He spat on the ground, made mud with His saliva, and anointed the man's eyes. Rather than using a grand display of power to heal, as many might have expected from the Messiah, Jesus chose to work through a humble and seemingly unremarkable act. The man was then instructed to wash in the Pool of Siloam, which required an act of obedience and faith on the man's part.

This healing was not just an act of physical restoration; it was a spiritual statement. It pointed to Jesus' mission, not as a political liberator or military leader, but as the Suffering Servant of God, who would bring light to the spiritually blind. The miracle itself was a symbolic act, revealing the deeper spiritual blindness of the religious leaders, who were unable to recognize the Messiah standing before them, even as they claimed to know the Scriptures.

The healing also drew sharp opposition from the Pharisees, who were scandalized not only by the act itself but by the fact that it took place on the Sabbath. For them, the Messiah would not defy the law in such a manner. Jesus' refusal to conform to these expectations—persisting on healing on the Sabbath, His focus on spiritual renewal over political deliverance—reveals His commitment to God's mission rather than to the religious or cultural expectations of the time.

In this narrative, we see Jesus not only healing physical blindness but revealing a larger truth about His identity and mission. He is the Light of the world (John 9:5), not as a political or military leader but as the One who brings sight to the spiritually blind, leading them into the true knowledge of God. His resistance to the political and societal pressures of His time, along with His choice to heal in ways that defy common expectations, underscores the central thesis of His ministry: He is the Suffering Servant who came to give His life as a ransom for many (Mark 10:45).

"The Light of the World"

He stood in dust and whispered prayer,
The blind man kneeling unaware,
Of all the worlds that stood in wait,
For healing, hope, and love to break.
With spit and mud, the work began,
The Word made flesh, the Son of Man,
He touched the eyes that saw no light,
And sent him to the pool that night.
"Go," He said, and trust My word,
And through the water, vision stirred.
The blind now saw with vision clear,

His soul awakened, filled with cheer.
For in this act, the truth unfurled,
The blind not only healed, but hurled
Into the Light, the Light of Life,
To see beyond this world's brief strife.
The Pharisees, in law's disguise,
Could not behold the open eyes,
For in their hearts, they could not see
The Truth that set the captives free.
And so He walked, unbowed, unbound,
A Suffering Servant, love unfound—
To heal the world, to take the blame,
And show us all the Father's name.
He healed the blind, He healed the soul,
He came to make the broken whole,
Not as a king, with sword or might,
But as the humble, patient Light.

Analysis:

The healing of the man born blind in John 9 serves as a poignant illustration of Jesus' resistance to the prevailing messianic expectations of His time. The people of Israel were largely looking for a political and military leader who would liberate them from Roman oppression. However, Jesus' ministry revealed that His mission was not political, nor was it centered on worldly power and glory. His acts of healing, especially this one, were not just about physical restoration but about a deeper spiritual awakening. Jesus, the Light of the world, came to open the eyes of the spiritually blind, to reveal the truth of God's kingdom, and to fulfill the role of the Suffering Servant of prophecy.

By healing the man on the Sabbath, Jesus also directly challenged the religious authorities' narrow and legalistic interpretations of what the Messiah should be and do. In this sense, the healing of the blind man was as much about exposing the spiritual blindness of Israel's leaders as it was about giving sight to the man. Jesus used this miracle to demonstrate that His kingdom would not come through conformity to the social or religious expectations of the time, but through the humble, sacrificial love of the Suffering Servant.

This event further underscores the broader theme of Jesus' resistance to the cultural and religious expectations of the Messiah. The healing points to the paradox of Jesus' mission: He came not to be served but to serve, not to wield earthly power but to lay down His life for the redemption of humanity. His mission was not defined by the need to conform to human expectations, but by His unwavering commitment to the will of the Father, to bring spiritual healing and salvation to a broken world. This is the heart of the gospel, and the healing of the blind man is a vivid portrayal of the light and life Jesus offers—light to those in spiritual darkness, and life through His ultimate act of sacrificial love.

Reflections

1. Jesus said the man's blindness was "*so that the works of God might be displayed in him.*" Where in your own life might suffering or difficulty be an opportunity for God's glory to be revealed?

2. The blind man obeyed Jesus' odd command—to wash mud from his eyes in a distant pool. When have you had to trust Jesus with something that didn't make sense at the time?

3. The religious leaders saw the miracle but refused to believe. In what ways might spiritual "blindness" still keep you—or others—from seeing what God is doing right in front of you?

39

The Royal Entry into Jerusalem

The Royal Entry of Jesus into Jerusalem, known today as Palm Sunday, is a pivotal moment that connects directly to Zechariah 9:9. As Jesus rode into the city on the colt of a donkey, He was not only fulfilling this prophecy but also participating in a deeply symbolic and royal act. In ancient Israel, the anointing of a king was often accompanied by a procession into the city, and the king would ride in on a horse if he were preparing for war, or on a donkey if he were coming in peace.

Jesus' choice of a donkey was no accident. He deliberately chose this humble animal, symbolizing peace and humility, to make a statement about the nature of His kingship. This was not the entrance of a military leader coming to overthrow an empire, but the entrance of a Savior coming to offer peace and salvation. As He rode into the city, the crowds enthusiastically spread palm branches before Him, a sign of respect and honor, traditionally reserved for victorious kings and rulers.

The people's expectations of the Messiah were tied to their hopes of a political deliverer. They were under Roman occupation and longed for a Messiah who would overthrow their oppressors and restore the kingdom of Israel. Their cries of *Hosanna!*—meaning *"Save us!"*—were a call for deliverance from Rome. But they did not fully understand that the salvation Jesus was bringing was not a political one, rather a spiritual one—deliverance from sin and death.

As Jesus entered Jerusalem, the contrast between His peaceful, humble nature and the crowds' expectations of a military conqueror was stark. This Royal Entry, while fulfilling Zechariah's prophecy, set the stage for the radical way in which Jesus would redefine what it meant to be the Messiah. He was a King who would not establish His kingdom through power and force, but through sacrifice, love, and the ultimate act of peace—His death on the cross.

"The Royal Entry"

O Zion, rejoice, your King has come,
Not in the storm, nor with the drum.
No chariot grand, no sword to wield,
But on a donkey, He enters the field.
Hosanna, they cry, with branches spread,
The King of Peace rides, though blood He'll shed.
The crowd expectant, their hearts full of cheer,
But the true victory was drawing near.
Not through a battle, not through might,
But by the cross, He brings the light.
Hosanna, they shout, with joy unrestrained,
Though they can't see He'll soon be slain.
O humble King, whose reign will last,
Through love and sacrifice, a kingdom vast.
A King of Peace, on this humble steed,
To meet our greatest, deepest need.

Analysis:

The Royal Entry of Jesus into Jerusalem marks the fulfillment of Zechariah 9:9 in a profound way. This prophecy was not just about a king's arrival—it was about the manner in which the King would come. The symbolism of Jesus' entry, riding on a donkey, was loaded with meaning: it directly contradicted the expectation of a militaristic, political Messiah who would come in power. Instead, Jesus demonstrated that His kingship was of a different order—one defined by peace, humility, and sacrifice.

This moment is a theological turning point in the Gospels. The crowds, waving palm branches and crying *Hosanna*, were reflecting their hope for deliverance, but their understanding of deliverance was limited. They sought freedom from Roman oppression, not realizing that Jesus had come to bring freedom from sin and death. This royal entry foreshadows the tension that would play out in the coming days as Jesus would confront the powers of this world, not with a sword, but with the power of sacrificial love.

Theologically, the Royal Entry also speaks to the nature of God's Kingdom. Jesus does not rule through domination or force; His reign is established through humility and grace. This contrasts sharply with the world's understanding of power. In this moment, Jesus redefines kingship and demonstrates the unexpected way in which God's salvation would unfold—through self-giving love, not violence or political maneuvering.

In the larger narrative of Scripture, this event connects to the broader theme of the "already but not yet" Kingdom of God. Jesus' entry into Jerusalem marks the arrival of the Kingdom, but the fullness of that Kingdom will not be realized until His death and resurrection. This moment on Palm Sunday anticipates the ultimate victory that Jesus will achieve through the cross, where His reign of peace will be fully established.

Conclusion:
The Royal Entry of Jesus into Jerusalem, fulfilling Zechariah 9:9, provides a striking contrast between the crowd's expectations of a political Messiah and the true nature of Jesus' kingship. It illustrates the tension between worldly notions of power and the divine plan of salvation. Through His humble, peaceful entry, Jesus revealed the heart of His mission: to bring peace, not through conquest, but through sacrifice. This moment, celebrated as Palm Sunday, not only fulfills prophecy but redefines what it means for Jesus to be the Messiah and King, shaping our understanding of God's Kingdom and His plan of redemption.

Reflections

1. The crowds cried "*Hosanna*," hoping Jesus would overthrow Rome. Have you ever hoped God would act in power, only to find He chose a path of peace instead? How did that shape your view of His Kingdom?

2. Jesus entered Jerusalem humbly on a donkey—not the warhorse many expected. What does His choice of humility over might reveal about His leadership—and how does it challenge our ideas of strength?

3. The disciples walked beside Jesus, still confused about what kind of king He was. When have you followed faithfully without fully understanding where Jesus was leading?

4. The Pharisees and religious leaders saw Jesus as a threat. In what ways do religious expectations still resist the radical grace and upside-down Kingdom Jesus brings?

5. Pilate and the Roman leaders dismissed Jesus as irrelevant—just another local prophet. Where in our world today is Jesus overlooked, not because of rejection, but because of indifference?

40

The Hour and the Kingdom

There was a moment at the Jordan River when time seemed to pause. Jesus, the Son of God, approached the waters with a quiet determination, despite the puzzling nature of the act itself. He had come to be baptized by John, a prophet who had called people to repentance. It must have seemed strange. After all, Jesus was without sin. And yet, in that moment, as He stepped into the river, He was fulfilling something deeper, something hidden from all but God.

Matthew's account gives us a glimpse of Jesus' perspective: *It is fitting for us to fulfill all righteousness* (Matt. 3:15). This moment was not just a ritual; it was an act laden with divine purpose. It was, as we now understand, the beginning of His mission to inaugurate the Kingdom of God. This was a sign that, at that point in time, God's plan for salvation and the restoration of His kingdom had reached its appointed hour. But this understanding of timing, this deep sense of "the moment," was not just an intellectual realization; it was an awareness rooted in revelation.

As Jesus walked through life, His awareness of time and purpose grew. He, in His humanity, was aware of moments that connected to the divine—conversations with Pharisees and confounding acts of kindness toward sinners and outcasts. These encounters revealed more than He could have known from His experience as a man. There were transcendent dimensions to His actions. The Father revealed what He needed to know, when He needed to know it.

One of the clearest examples was His conversation with the Samaritan woman. Jesus revealed to her the depths of her life in a way that no human could have known—five husbands and a lover—

and she marveled that He could know these things. Jesus would later state that He spoke only what the Father revealed to Him (John 8:26). That He spoke just what the Father taught Him (John 8:28).

As the Gospels unfold, especially in John, we begin to see that Jesus' "hour" had not yet come, but His life was a continual unveiling of God's purposes, a supernatural rhythm revealed through His daily encounters. His sense of timing was not simply based on human experience or the passage of days; it was based on the same divine revelation as His exchange with the woman at the well.

In John 2:4, when He told His mother, *My hour has not yet come*, it was not just a casual statement. Jesus knew that there was a divine rhythm to His mission—one that transcended the understanding of His disciples or others around Him. His mission, like the moment at the Jordan River, was moving toward an inevitable climax: the cross, where He would take on the sins of the world and establish God's eternal Kingdom.

And then, as His death drew near, He uttered the words that would forever mark the turning of the ages: *The hour has come* (John 12:23). The Greek God-fearers who were in Jerusalem to worship desired an audience with Jesus (John 12:20-21). It appears that He did not grant that audience. But something in their request made Jesus declare that His hour had come.

That hour was not merely a moment on the clock. It was a convergence of heaven and earth, of divine will and human agency, of past prophecy and present fulfillment. The death of Jesus would not simply be the tragic death of a righteous man; it would be the defining act in the restoration of God's Kingdom—a Kingdom that, though still misunderstood, would begin to unfold through His resurrection and the coming of the Holy Spirit.

At His Ascension, when the disciples asked, *Lord, will you at this time restore the kingdom to Israel?* (Acts 1:6), they still could not understand. Jesus' Kingdom was not a geopolitical power; it was a spiritual reign inaugurated by His death and would be made manifest through the indwelling of the Holy Spirit in His followers. Jesus' response (Acts 1:7), affirmed that there was a transcendent aspect to God's Kingdom, one that could not be comprehended in human terms, but would only be understood by the power of the Spirit.

The "hour" that Jesus so frequently referenced—His hour—was the precise, divinely ordained moment that would not only fulfill prophecy but also establish the Kingdom of God in a way the world had not anticipated. This was not a Kingdom of armies and dominion, but a Kingdom of the cross, where the King would lay down His life for His people.

"The Hour Has Come"

The hour has come, the world will see,
A King who comes not to decree
A throne of gold, a scepter bright,
But through the dark of endless night.
His kingdom's not of land or stone,
But of the heart, by grace begun.
The Father's will, His life will show,
And through His death, the Kingdom grows.
The cross, the crown, the blood, the cry,
The moment when the King must die.
For in that hour, the world is changed,
And all we've known is rearranged.
The truth is told from earth to sky,
The seed is planted, it must die.
The hour has come, the time is near,
God's reign begins with hearts sincere.

Analysis: The Transcendence of God in the Hour

The concept of "the hour" in the Gospels, particularly in John, is intimately connected to the transcendence of God. The Father, who exists outside of time and space, orchestrates history with perfect precision. Jesus' understanding of His mission and the timing of His death is not a result of human calculation but a divine revelation. It's this transcendence that sets the context for the Kingdom of God that Jesus came to establish.

At the Ascension, Jesus pointed His disciples beyond their immediate questions about national restoration to the broader picture of God's sovereign will. The Kingdom He was inaugurating would not be bound by earthly kingdoms, political agendas, or national borders. It would be a Kingdom that transcended these limitations, grounded in the power of the Holy Spirit and the work of Christ on the cross.

Jesus' "hour" is not simply a moment in history. It is the confluence of eternity and time—the appointed moment in God's eternal plan where history pivots. The transcendence of God is visible here: God, in His infinite wisdom, orchestrates the redemption of the world, not through the means that humans would choose, but through the paradox of the cross. Through His death, God would establish His reign in the hearts of those who would believe, drawing them into a Kingdom that was already present in seed form but would fully unfold through the coming of the Spirit.

This transcendent aspect of God's work also teaches us something critical about His timing. We live in a world where the seasons of life unfold in patterns we can anticipate, but God's plans are far more mysterious. As Jesus' disciples learned in Acts 1:7, God's timing for the restoration of all things is His alone to know.

The Kingdom is now, through the Spirit, but it will be fully realized in God's perfect time, according to His will. This should humble us as we seek to understand our role in God's redemptive plan. We are participants in the unfolding Kingdom, but we must trust God's timing, knowing that our understanding is limited and our efforts will only bear fruit according to His purpose.

Woven together is the significance of time and revelation in

Jesus' life, the transcendent nature of God's Kingdom, and the divine timing of Jesus' death to establish that Kingdom. Jesus recognized the moment. He was able to separate the signal from the noise. And when the moment came, Jesus recognized it and acted.

Structured around Jesus' sense of time, the transcendence of God, and the Kingdom of God—especially focusing on the concepts of divine revelation, timing, and the nature of Jesus' mission, we have the sense that God has been orchestrating the events and moments of Jesus' life. And He works in our lives to do the same thing—if only we can separate the signal from the noise.

Reflections

1. Jesus often spoke of His "*hour*" not yet arriving—until suddenly, it had. Have you ever sensed that God was preparing you for something, even if you couldn't name it yet? How do you discern when your "hour" has come—or when it hasn't?

2. From His baptism to the cross, Jesus walked in step with the Father's will. What does His example teach you about the pace and path of spiritual obedience?

3. God's Kingdom often unfolds quietly—through obscure towns, unexpected people, and suffering rather than strength. Where in your life might the Kingdom be taking root in quiet, unseen ways?

4. Jesus' journey was marked by divine timing, not human expectation. How might trusting God's timing reshape the way you respond to frustration, delay, or confusion?

5. This vignette closes a chapter—from Galilee to Jerusalem, from hiddenness to public confrontation. As you look back through the life of Jesus (and the journey of this book), what have you seen more clearly? What themes or truths have emerged for you along the way?

Journaling: The Hour Has Come

Take a few moments to reflect on the arc of Jesus' life—from the moment He stepped into the Jordan River until the moment He entered Jerusalem. Through each vignette, we've followed Him—not just geographically, but spiritually. We've watched the Kingdom unfold in surprising, often upside-down ways.

1. What has surprised you most about the way Jesus lived and led?

2. Where has your understanding of the Kingdom grown or been challenged?

3. What "hour" might God be preparing you for? How are you being called to readiness—even if the moment hasn't yet arrived?

A Prayer for the Journey

Jesus, You walked through life with a sacred awareness of the moment.
You were never hurried, never aimless—You moved in step with the Father's will.
Teach me to do the same.
Help me trust the seasons I don't yet understand.
Give me eyes to see Your Kingdom unfolding, even when it defies my expectations.
And when my hour comes—whatever that may be—
Give me courage to act, and peace to rest in Your timing.

Amen.

41

Cleansing the Temple
A Clash of Kingdoms

Jesus entered the temple with a righteous zeal, and what He found there was a stark contradiction to the sacred purpose of the space. Merchants were buying and selling. Money changers were exchanging coins for the temple tax. The air was thick—not with prayer—but with commerce. The temple, meant to be a house of prayer, had become a den of thieves. With decisive action, Jesus overturned the tables and drove out those who had made His Father's house a marketplace.

His words rang out with prophetic force: *It is written, 'My house shall be called a house of prayer,' but you make it a den of robbers* (Matthew 21:13). Jesus was not simply addressing physical corruption; He was confronting a system that had turned worship into profit and excluded the poor and vulnerable.

In the wake of this dramatic moment, something remarkable happened. The blind and the lame—those often marginalized—were brought to Jesus. In contrast to the exploitation He had just condemned, Jesus responded with compassion. He healed them, offering a glimpse of the temple's true purpose: restoration, not revenue. Then the children began crying out, *"Hosanna to the Son of David!"* Their words, rich with messianic meaning, stirred the tension even further. *"Son of David"* was a bold declaration that Jesus was the promised Messiah, and the religious leaders recognized it as a direct challenge to their authority and to their money laundering schemes. What others saw as innocent praise, they perceived as threat.

The high priests and scribes, along with the Pharisees, Sadducees, and Herodians, saw Jesus as a danger to the fragile order they had worked to preserve. The temple was central to their power, and Jesus was disrupting it. The growing recognition of Him as Messiah threatened both their religious control and political alliances.

When the leaders confronted Jesus, demanding that He silence the children, He replied, *"Yes; have you never read, 'Out of the mouth of infants and nursing babies you have prepared praise'?"* (Matt. 21:16). By quoting Psalm 8:2, He affirmed that their praises were not only appropriate—they were divinely ordained. Even in the voice of children, the Kingdom was speaking.

By allowing and affirming their cries, Jesus was publicly accepting the title of Messiah. The cleansing of the temple was more than protest; it was a prophetic act that pointed to the need for systemic renewal. He had not come to support the old order, but to fulfill it—and establish something entirely new.

The cleansing, the healing, the messianic praise—they all pointed to a kingdom built not on power or politics, but on mercy, justice, and truth. And for the leaders, that meant only one thing: Jesus had to be removed.

"Hosanna to the Son of David"

In the temple courts, a holy cry,
Hosanna, to the Son, they cried!
A king had come, not with sword in hand,
But with healing touch, a servant's stand.
"Son of David!" the children proclaimed,
While the priests in anger quietly blamed.
The tables overturned, the coins did fall,
A kingdom reformed, not by might, but call.
A house of prayer, no longer a den,
The Messiah had come, the time was then.
The blind and the lame were healed anew,
Restored what once was pure and true.
But the leaders, in fear and in pride,

Saw their power threatened, could not abide.
"Silence them, Lord," they did demand,
But Jesus answered with God's own command:
"Out of babes, praise is due My name,
The kingdom is here, the world will change."

Analysis: "Son of David" and the Escalating Conflict

The title *Son of David* was more than genealogical—it was a loaded messianic claim. The children's cries were a public declaration that Jesus was the Anointed One, the fulfillment of God's promises to Israel. For the religious leaders, this was dangerous.

Jesus' acceptance of the title—and His use of Psalm 8 to defend it—was more than bold. It was revelatory. God's kingdom had arrived, not in the power centers of the elite, but in the humble and innocent voices of children.

The temple cleansing was not merely symbolic judgment; it was a prelude to a greater reckoning. Jesus was fulfilling the Law, redefining the sacred space, and becoming the new center of worship. His kingdom would not be built on systems of control, but on lives transformed by grace.

This episode was not just confrontation—it was culmination. The lines were drawn. And the road to the cross had begun.

Reflections

Jesus cleansed the temple not just with force, but with purpose. He healed, welcomed, and affirmed the children's praise—all while standing against corruption and hypocrisy.

1. In what ways is Jesus still overturning tables today—in your own heart, in the church, or in the world around you?

2. The children saw what the priests could not. How might you cultivate a childlike openness to God's presence and voice?

Journaling: A Temple Turned Over

The temple was the heart of Israel's worship, yet it had drifted from its purpose. Jesus didn't simply critique it—He stepped in and cleared the space. He made room again for prayer, healing, and true praise.

As you reflect on this moment:

Are there areas in your life where clutter or compromise has crept into spaces meant for communion with God?

What needs to be overturned, driven out, or restored in your spiritual rhythms?

Who have you been tempted to exclude—those Jesus might instead be welcoming to His table?

What praise—genuine, unfiltered—might rise from you if space were cleared?

Let your journal become the courtyard. Let Jesus walk through it. Ask Him what stays, what must go, and what is waiting to be healed.

You might close your journaling with a prayer:

Jesus, cleanse my heart. Drive out what doesn't belong. Make me a house of prayer again. And let my praise rise—not from habit or ritual, but from wonder, from truth, from love. Amen.

42

The Widow's Wealth
(Mark 12:41–44; Luke 21:1–4)

The clink of coins echoed through the Temple courts. Wealthy men passed by the treasury chests, their offerings a display of generosity—impressive to the ear, if not the soul. The disciples, perhaps like most, were drawn to the grandeur. Surely these were the benefactors of God's house.

But Jesus' eyes were fixed elsewhere.

A widow moved quietly through the crowd. She came with no fanfare, no retinue, no outward significance. She reached the offering box and dropped in two small copper coins. They barely made a sound. But Heaven heard the thunder of her gift.

Jesus called His disciples close—not to praise the philanthropists, but to honor the widow.

"Truly I tell you," He said, *"this poor widow has put in more than all the others. They gave out of their wealth; she gave out of her poverty—all she had to live on."*

This is the strange arithmetic of the Kingdom.

Here, value isn't measured by what is given, but by what remains. Sacrifice, not surplus, reveals the heart. To the watching world, her gift was forgettable. To the King, it was unforgettable. And centuries later, it still echoes—two small coins that outweighed empires.

"Kingdom Accounting"
She passed the courts where silver rang,
Where pride and purse in chorus sang.
No retinue, no wealthy name,

A soul alight, no claim to fame
Two copper coins—a widow's wealth,
No surplus stored, no hidden stealth.
She gave not what she wouldn't miss,
But all she had—her life, her bliss.
The watchers saw no grand display,
But Jesus watched a different way.
He counted not the gold or gem,
But love that overflowed from them.
The ledgers tallied loud and bright,
But one gift rose in Heaven's sight.
For in the Kingdom, weight is shown
By what remains when we have sown.
So give, not just from what you hold—
But from the place where faith is bold.
For Heaven hears the smallest sound
When Kingdom hearts in trust abound.

Reflections

1. What does Jesus' praise of the widow's offering reveal about how God measures generosity? How does this contrast with the way our culture—and even the church—evaluates giving?

2. Why do you think the disciples needed to be taught this lesson? What assumptions about wealth, influence, or spiritual value might they (or we) have carried into that moment?

3. How should this passage inform our view of modern Christian leadership and stewardship—especially in an age of megachurches, celebrity pastors, and prosperity preaching?

4. Is there a place for public generosity? What's the line between faithful stewardship and self-promotion?

5. How can we cultivate a spirit of giving that reflects the widow's heart—giving generously with trust in God?

43

The Rejected Stone

It was a tense morning in the Temple courtyard. Jesus had entered the heart of Jerusalem, the city He had longed to visit, and the air buzzed with anticipation. As He began to teach the people, the chief priests and the elders of the people, the very men who were supposed to be guiding Israel, came to Him. Their question was sharp and accusatory:

"By what authority are You doing these things? Who gave You this authority?" (Matthew 21:23).

They had come not to learn but to trap. Their minds were set on one thing—discrediting this Teacher who was challenging their authority, who had overturned the money changers' tables and disturbed the delicate balance of power in the Temple.

But Jesus, as He always did, recognized their ploy. He turned the tables on them, responding with a question of His own:
"I will also ask you one question, and if you tell Me the answer, then I will also tell you by what authority I do these things. The baptism of John, from where did it come? From heaven or from men?"
(Matthew 21:24-25).

They huddled together, weighing the implications. To say "from heaven" would mean they had to explain why they had rejected John's message. To say "from men" would risk the wrath of the people, who regarded John as a prophet. So they gave the only answer that would not compromise them: *"We do not know."*

Jesus, with a knowing glance, replied: *"Neither will I tell you by what authority I do these things."*

But He did not stop there. He knew their hearts. He knew their pride. And so He told them two parables that exposed their hypocrisy and revealed their misunderstanding of the Kingdom of God.

In the first, the parable of the two sons (Matthew 21:28-32), Jesus described a father who asked his two sons to work in the vineyard. One son said he would go but did not; the other said he would not but later went. Jesus asked them, *"Which of the two did the will of his father?"* The answer was clear: the son who repented and went, despite his initial refusal. The point was stark: the tax collectors and prostitutes—those whom the religious leaders despised— were entering the Kingdom of God before they would.

In the second, the parable of the wicked tenants (Matthew 21:33 -41), Jesus told of a landowner who entrusted his vineyard to tenants. When he sent his servants to collect the fruit of the vineyard, they were beaten and killed by the tenants. Finally, he sent his son, and they killed him too. Jesus asked, *"What will the owner of the vineyard do to those tenants?"* The answer was judgment. He would take the vineyard away and give it to others who would produce the fruit. The Jewish leaders were enraged. They recognized that Jesus was speaking about them—those who had been entrusted with God's people and had failed to bring forth the fruit of righteousness.

Then Jesus quoted from Psalm 118:22-23:
"The stone that the builders rejected has become the cornerstone. This is the Lord's doing, and it is marvelous in our eyes" (Matthew 21:42).

He was the stone, the rejected stone, the one whom they would soon reject entirely. But in their rejection, He would become the cornerstone of a new kingdom, a kingdom not built on the power and pride of men but on the sacrifice and righteousness of God.

And Jesus declared, *"Therefore I tell you, the kingdom of God will be taken away from you and given to a people producing its fruits."* (Matthew 21:43). The Jewish leadership's rejection of Jesus, the Messiah, would lead to the transfer of the kingdom to those who would respond to Him in faith—those who would become the *ekkle-sia*, the church, the new chosen people of God (1 Peter 2:9-10).

"The Stone Rejected"

They came with questions, sharp and keen,
To trap, to test, to intervene.
"By what authority do You speak?
Who sent You, Teacher, strong yet meek?"
But Jesus saw through veils of pride,
And with a question, turned the tide:
"John's baptism—tell Me true—
Was it from heaven, or man-made too?"
They stalled and stumbled in their shame,
Caught in their plots, they dared not name
The truth, the way, the One to know—
And so the Teacher let them go.
Then with two stories, clear and strong,
He showed them where they'd gone so wrong:
The son who turned, the tenants vile—
Their hearts were hard, their ways defiled.
"The stone the builders cast aside
Will be the cornerstone, firm with pride.
The Kingdom's gates will open wide
To those who come, with hearts untied."
The Kingdom taken, not yet lost—
A people born through blood-bought cost.
The Stone rejected—now our King,
He reigns in love—come, rise and sing.

Analysis:

This encounter between Jesus and the Jewish leaders serves as a profound turning point in the narrative of the Gospels. Jesus skillfully navigates their traps, revealing not only their misunderstanding of His authority but also the nature of the Kingdom He was bringing.

By quoting Psalm 118:22-23, Jesus identified Himself as the rejected stone, a cornerstone that would be the foundation of a new people, a new Kingdom. His rejection by the religious leaders and the Jewish nation as a whole set the stage for the inclusion of the Gentiles and the creation of the church, the new *ekklesia*.

The parables Jesus tells—the two sons and the wicked tenants—serve as critiques of Israel's leadership, showing how those entrusted with God's mission failed to bear the fruit He desired. In these stories, the religious elite are shown to be like the first son who said he would obey but did not, and like the wicked tenants who rejected and killed the messengers sent by the landowner.

By the end of this encounter, the leaders' rejection of Jesus becomes clear. And His declaration that the Kingdom will be taken from them and given to another people is both a judgment and a prophesy. It points forward to the birth of the church, a people who would respond to Jesus' call and bear the fruit of righteousness.

Ultimately, this vignette reveals the deep theological truth that Jesus is the true cornerstone of God's Kingdom, a Kingdom not of this world but one that will endure forever. The rejection He faced is central to understanding the contrast between the world's expectations of power and the true power of the Kingdom of God. Through His rejection, Jesus became the foundation upon which the church would be built, and in His resurrection, the true authority of the Kingdom would be fully revealed.

Reflections

For Jesus, professing the Kingdom required producing its fruit.

1. Where in your life is God asking you not just to profess faith—but to produce fruit?

2. Are there areas where pride or complacency might be keeping you from fully embracing His authority?

3. What would it look like to build your life on the cornerstone the world still tends to reject?

44

The Anointing and The Betrayal

It was the evening before the storm. The final days were fast approaching, and the air in Jerusalem seemed thick with anticipation. Jesus had gathered with His disciples in the house of Simon the leper in Bethany. The room held the murmur of conversation, the scent of a simple meal, and the quiet presence of the One who had shown the world a Kingdom unlike any other. Then something unexpected happened.

Mary, the sister of Lazarus, broke through the gathering with a costly jar of perfume, a spikenard ointment, and in an act that would forever be etched into the Gospel story, she poured it over Jesus' head. The fragrance filled the room—a lavish display of love, devotion, and worship. Jesus, with a knowing smile, accepted the offering, saying, *"She has done a beautiful thing to me. In pouring this ointment on my body, she has done it to prepare me for burial"* (Matthew 26:10-12). In her anointing, Mary—unlike many others—seemed to recognize the true purpose of Jesus' mission. His death was near, and she was honoring Him as the Suffering Servant, the One who would give His life.

As she knelt at His feet, the disciples murmured in disapproval. *"Why this waste?"* they said, as the perfume could have been sold for a great price, and the money given to the poor (Matthew 26:8). But Jesus, patient and discerning, gently rebuked them. *"Why do you trouble her? She has done a good thing for me. For you always have the poor with you, but you will not always have me"* (Matthew 26:10-11). Mary's actions were not just an expression of worship;

they were a prophetic declaration of the love and sacrifice that would soon be poured out on the cross.

But outside, another act was unfolding—a stark contrast to Mary's. As Mary anointed Jesus, Judas Iscariot, one of the Twelve, slipped quietly away. Driven by his greed, his disillusionment, or perhaps some misguided expectation that Jesus would rise to power if His hand was forced, Judas went to the chief priests. *"What will you give me if I deliver him over to you?"* (Matthew 26:15). The deal was struck: thirty pieces of silver, the price of a slave, was all that Judas would receive for betraying his Master.

The clash of these two responses could not be more pronounced. Mary's extravagant love for Jesus, her act of worship, stood in stark contrast to Judas' betrayal, motivated by greed and the disillusionment of unmet expectations. Mary understood Jesus' true mission, even though His disciples had yet to fully comprehend it. Judas, on the other hand, was looking for a different kind of Messiah—one who would overthrow the Roman oppressors and establish an earthly kingdom. When he saw that Jesus was not that Messiah, Judas turned away, selling his loyalty for thirty pieces of silver.

"Two Choices"

In a room filled with scent, precious and pure,
A woman knelt low, her love to assure.
A jar was broken, fragrance ascended,
Anointing the One whose death was intended.
The disciples protested, "The cost is too great!"
But Jesus replied, "She's sees My fate.
Her act of devotion prepares Me for death—
A burial soon, with My final breath."
But in the shadows, a dark plot stirred—
Judas, the traitor, betrayed with a word.
He sold the Lord for silver, cheap—
A kiss for a King, a moment to weep.

Two hearts, two choices, in one fateful night:
One chose love's beauty; the other, the fight.
One saw the Savior—Messiah, the King;
The other saw loss, a broken thing.

Analysis

The contrast between Mary's anointing and Judas' betrayal high-lights the different ways people responded to Jesus' identity and mission. Mary's act of worship was an acknowledgment of Jesus' true purpose as the Suffering Servant, while Judas' betrayal reflected his deep misunderstanding of who Jesus was, what He had come to do, and what He came to establish.

Mary, in her humble act of anointing Jesus, expressed a recognition that others, including the disciples, had failed to grasp. Jesus had been trying to explain His impending death to them, but they were focused on political expectations—on the coming Kingdom that would overthrow Rome and restore Israel. But Mary understood that Jesus' true mission was not to bring a temporary earthly kingdom, but to lay down His life for the salvation of the world. Her anointing was not a frivolous act but a prophetic gesture of devotion, a recognition of His coming death, and a preparation for His burial.

In contrast, Judas' motivations for betrayal remain shrouded in mystery. Whether driven by greed, disappointment, or an unmet desire for Jesus to act as the political deliverer he had hoped for, Judas' decision to betray Jesus was marked by the same selfishness that had been evident in his life for years. John reveals that Judas was a thief (John 12:6), and his heart was inclined toward personal gain. Judas' rejection of Jesus as the true Messiah—one who would die as the Lamb for the sins of the world—was the final act of his spiritual blindness. Having been with Jesus for years, His betrayal shocked.

What is especially poignant is that both Mary and Judas were physically close to Jesus. Mary understood Jesus' heart and respond-ed in an act of extravagant love, while Judas, having followed Jesus for three years, could not see past his own desires and ended up betraying Him for a paltry sum. This moment forces us to ask: How do we respond to Jesus? Do we, like Mary, recognize His true mission and offer our lives in devotion, or do we, like Judas, misinterpret His purpose and ultimately turn away, seeking our own agendas?

The mystery of Judas' motivations and his eventual remorse leading to his tragic end, serve as a reminder of the devastating consequences of rejecting the true nature of Jesus' Kingdom. This illustrates the profound spiritual conflict that Jesus faced in the final days of His life, as well as the different ways in which people reacted to His offer of salvation: some in adoration, others in rejection.

Reflections

1. Mary offered something costly, beautiful, and deeply personal—her gift was love expressed without holding back. What would an offering like that look like in your life today? Where might Jesus be inviting you to pour something precious at His feet?

2. The disciples called Mary's act "waste," but Jesus called it "beautiful." Are there ways your love for Christ—or someone else's—has been misunderstood, questioned, or dismissed? How does Jesus' response affirm the quiet, unseen acts of devotion?

3. Judas and Mary both stood close to Jesus—but only one truly saw Him. What keeps us from seeing Jesus clearly? Are there expectations, disappointments, or distractions that might be clouding your own vision of who He really is?

4. Mary acted in love; Judas acted in self-interest. What subtle forms of self-serving faith might we carry, even while walking with Jesus? Where is the Spirit prompting you toward deeper surrender?

5. Jesus said Mary's act would be remembered wherever the gospel is preached. Why do you think He honored her in this way? How does her example shape your understanding of legacy—not of fame or accomplishment, but of sacrificial love and lasting faithfulness?

45

The Surrender in Gethsemane

In the quiet of the garden, Jesus experienced anguish unlike any other. This was not the confident stride of a conquering Messiah. What unfolded in Gethsemane was a raw, deeply human moment. The eternal *Logos*, self-limited in human form, now faced the reality of what was to come: betrayal, arrest, mocking, brutal suffering, and death on a cross. Could there be another way?

He came to pray, to commune with the Father, and to wrestle with the cup before Him. The weight of sin and the horror of the cross pressed upon His soul. The Gospels tell us His soul was *"very sorrowful, even to death"*—a stark contrast to the composure we might expect from divine authority.

Three times He prayed for the cup to pass—not seeking escape, but asking, in His humanity, whether another way might fulfill the Father's will. Yet each time, He returned to the words of surrender: *"Nevertheless, not as I will, but as You will."* Jesus, in His full humanity, made the choice to submit His will to the Father's plan, despite the excruciating cost. This was not divine inevitability but chosen obedience.

The writer of Hebrews reflected this moment, noting that Jesus *"learned obedience through what He suffered."* His obedience was not easy or automatic; it was forged through agony. The cost was shown through the depth of His struggle, through His willingness to face suffering and not turn away from it. Jesus' obedience, even in His most vulnerable state, became the gateway for the salvation of all who would follow Him. This moment of sin-bearing and sacrifice foreshadowed in the Day of Atonement had arrived. He knew all of history had come to this moment for this purpose—redemption.

In this moment, Jesus was not simply fulfilling a divine mandate from the safety of His omnipotence. He had laid that aside. He faced His death with dread and modeled for us the way of surrender. Trusting the Father's will above all, He chose God's path over His own desires.

"The Cup and the Cross"

In the garden, 'neath the olive tree,
A man in sorrow, on bended knee,
Cries out in grief, His heart undone,
As shadowed thoughts of death now come.
The cup before Him, filled with strife—
A bitter draught of death and life.
He pleads, "If there's another way,
Let this dark burden pass today."
"Father, take this cup from Me—
If it be Your will," His earnest plea.
But in the hush, no voice replies,
And still He prays, with tear-stained eyes.
Three times He asks, yet each time yields,
To trust in God—the battle sealed.
"Not My will, but Yours be done"—
The struggle ends, the fight is won.
For through the silence, pain, and loss,
He bears the weight, He bears the cross.
And from that place of deepest woe,
A Savior's love begins to flow.

Analysis: The Humanity of Jesus in the Garden

In the Garden of Gethsemane, we are given a powerful window into the humanity of Jesus. This is a moment of vulnerability, of intense emotion, and of struggle. Jesus chose to live within the limitations of His humanity. He was not merely an automaton moving toward His death but a man who, in the fullest sense, felt the weight of what He was about to face. Just moments later, at the betrayal, Jesus said He could have asked the Father for twelve legions of angels—and been delivered. But He did not. That's surrender.

The fact that Jesus prayed for the cup to pass indicates the depth of His human experience. He felt fear, sorrow, and hesitation— emotions that are not foreign to us, and yet He faced them with an unwavering commitment to God's will. This prayer demonstrates that His sinlessness was not the result of some divine immunity from human struggle but was a product of His conscious, willful choice to align Himself with the Father's plan, even when it was painful.

In Hebrews 5:7-9, the writer clarifies that Jesus' obedience was "*learned*" through His suffering. This doesn't mean that Jesus lacked knowledge or that His divine nature was incomplete, but rather that in His humanity, He was experiencing the process of submission and trust that is required of all believers.

His obedience, wrought through pain and surrender, became the foundation of our salvation. His human struggle was not weakness— it was the necessary path of redemption. It was through this very struggle that He became "*the source of eternal salvation*" for all who obey Him.

Jesus' actions in Gethsemane challenge our own understanding of obedience and submission. In a world where personal will and autonomy are so often prioritized, Jesus offers a radically different example. His submission to the Father's will was not easy or painless, but it was through this moment of surrender that the Kingdom of God was inaugurated. It is in this model of obedience—choosing God's will above personal desire—that we are invited to follow.

For Christians, Gethsemane is both a moment of awe and a call to action. It demonstrates that obedience to God is not about perfect performance but about trust in God's goodness and sovereignty.

Even in our own struggles—facing fear, uncertainty, or the cost of obedience—we are called to echo His prayer: "*Not my will, but Yours be done.*"

Reflections

In Gethsemane, we see not only the suffering Savior but the surrendered Son. He did not rush toward the cross with unfeeling resolve. He knelt, He wept, He wrestled—and then, He yielded.

1. Jesus prayed three times for the cup to pass, yet each time He returned to surrender. Where in your life have you prayed for something to change—but God has invited you to trust Him instead?

2. Obedience did not come easily for Jesus—it came through struggle. How does that truth reshape your view of your own struggles with surrender?

Journaling: Not My Will

This moment in the garden was not the absence of faith—but the cost of it. Jesus chose the harder path not because He felt no fear, but because He trusted the Father's heart more than His own desire.

Where in your life is God inviting you to say, *"Not my will, but Yours be done"*?

Are there areas of fear, uncertainty, or resistance that need to be brought honestly before Him?

What would it look like to trust that even the hard path—if it is His path—can become holy ground?

Close in a simple prayer of surrender, in your words, or echo His: *"Father, not my will, but Yours be done. In weakness, be my strength. In fear, be my peace. In hesitation, be my courage. Amen."*

46

The Kangaroo Court

The night was dark, and the air thick with tension. After the events in the Garden of Gethsemane, where Judas had betrayed Jesus with a kiss, Jesus was bound and brought before the very leaders who had sought His destruction. The high priests and the elders of the people, the very ones who had questioned His authority just days earlier in the Temple, now held a mock trial in the house of the high priest, Caiaphas. This was no ordinary trial. It was a kangaroo court—a sham of justice bent on condemning Jesus at all costs .

Matthew's account is stark. *"Those who had seized Jesus led him to Caiaphas the high priest, where the scribes and the elders had gathered"* (Matthew 26:57). These were the religious authorities of Israel, the men entrusted with the spiritual welfare of the people. And yet, their hearts were clouded by greed, envy, and a thirst for power.

They were desperate to rid themselves of this troublemaker, this man who had been turning the world upside down. Jesus, the carpenter's son from Nazareth, had claimed to be the Messiah, the Anointed One, the promised King. But He was not the political, militaristic ruler they had envisioned. He did not come to overthrow Rome in a blaze of glory; instead, He spoke of a Kingdom that was not of this world, a Kingdom defined by humility, service, and sacrifice.

As the trial began, the high priest and the council tried to find false witnesses who would testify against Jesus. *"But they found none, though many false witnesses came forward"* (Matthew 26:60).

No charge would stick. Their desperation grew, and finally, two men came forward and accused Jesus of claiming to destroy the Temple and rebuild it in three days. It was a misrepresentation of His words, but it was enough to provide a semblance of accusation.

The high priest's eyes burned with accusation as he turned to Jesus. *"Have you no answer to make? What is it that these men testify against you?"* (Matthew 26:62). But Jesus remained silent. The silence spoke volumes—He did not need to defend Himself against these unjust charges. He was the spotless Lamb, the innocent One, standing before a corrupt court. And what good would it do?

Finally, the high priest, exasperated and desperate, put Jesus under oath. *"I adjure you by the living God, tell us if you are the Christ, the Son of God"* (Matthew 26:63). The question was clear, and it was a trap. If Jesus confessed, they could accuse Him of blasphemy and call for His death; if He remained silent, they could twist His silence into an admission of guilt.

But Jesus, with unflinching resolve, answered, *"You have said so. But I tell you, from now on you will see the Son of Man seated at the right hand of Power and coming on the clouds of heaven"* (Mt. 26:64). In these words, Jesus declared His identity as the Messiah, not in the way they expected, but in a way that pointed to His ultimate authority as the Son of Man who would come in glory to judge the living and the dead.

At these words, the high priest tore his clothes in outrage, declaring, *"He has uttered blasphemy. What further witnesses do we need? You have now heard His blasphemy. What is your judgment?"* (Matthew 26:65). They answered with one voice, *"He deserves death."* The verdict was sealed.

The religious leaders were blind. Their greed for power and their desire to maintain control over the people had clouded their ability to see the truth. Jesus was not the Messiah they wanted—He was not the political warrior who would bring Israel back to prominence. He was the suffering Servant, the Lamb who would take away the sins of the world, and they could not understand Him.

"So You Say"

In the darkened halls of power,
They schemed to end His final hour.
False witnesses with twisted lies,
But truth stood still, before their eyes.
The Lamb was silent, bound by love,
No plea for rescue from above.
The cries of rage rang loud and raw,
Yet He denied no crown, no law.
The priest tore garments, heart ablaze,
"Blasphemy!" he dared to raise.
"Are You the Christ, the chosen One?"
The room grew still—He would not run.
"You say I am," He spoke with grace,
No sword in hand, no fear to face.
"The Son of Man you soon shall see,
On heaven's clouds, in majesty."
But they were blind, they would not know,
Their hearts were hard, their hate would grow.
The Stone rejected, scorned, despised—
Will rise to rule, and open eyes.

Analysis

The trial before the high priest and the Sanhedrin is one of the darkest moments in the Gospel narrative, as it reveals the deep corruption and misunderstanding of the religious leadership. Here, Jesus is questioned not as a teacher or healer, but as a threat to the established order. The Sanhedrin, in their pursuit of power and control, fail to recognize the true Messiah standing before them. They were not interested in truth; they sought only to protect their own positions of influence.

The trial reveals the fundamental conflict of the Gospel—Jesus came not to uphold the status quo but to usher in a radically different Kingdom. The religious leaders, blinded by their greed and thirst for power, could not grasp the nature of the Kingdom Jesus proclaimed. They wanted a political Messiah who would deliver Israel from Roman oppression, but Jesus offered a spiritual Kingdom that challenged the very fabric of their authority and financial schemes.

When Jesus declares Himself to be the Christ, the Son of God, and the Son of Man seated at the right hand of Power, He is asserting His divine authority. But this authority is not exercised through military might or political maneuvers; it is a divine authority that will be revealed through His suffering, death, and resurrection. Jesus' declaration points to the reality that His Kingdom is not of this world, and it will come in glory, in a manner that the religious leaders cannot yet comprehend.

The irony of the trial is striking: the very people who should have recognized the Messiah are the ones who condemn Him. This blindness is at the heart of the rejection of Jesus—an inability to see the true nature of God's plan for salvation. Their misunderstanding of the Messiah is a tragedy, but it also sets the stage for the unfolding of God's redemptive work through Jesus' sacrificial death and triumphant resurrection.

The clash between earthly power and divine authority is laid bare. Their rejection of Jesus, rooted in misconceptions of the Messiah, stands as a sobering reminder of the danger of clinging to worldly power and resisting the call to recognize Jesus as the true King of the Kingdom of God.

Reflections

1. When have you needed the courage to remain faithful and quiet in the face of misunderstanding or injustice?
2. What preconceived ideas or fears might keep us from seeing Jesus as He truly is—and following where He leads?

47

Before Pilate

The time had come. The "hour" that Jesus had so often referenced in His ministry was now upon Him. The shadow of the cross loomed large as He stood before Pontius Pilate, the Roman governor. In this moment, all the expectations of those around Him, from the religious elite to the Roman authorities, clashed with the divine plan that Jesus was fulfilling. The situation was complex—entangled with politics, religion, and misconceptions about the Messiah.

Pilate's question, *Are you the King of the Jews?* (John 18:33) reflected the secular, earthly understanding of kingship—power, dominance, and authority in the traditional sense. To claim kingship would have been treason against Caesar, and Pilate, as a Roman official, was fully aware of the political implications. Yet Jesus' response was simple and profound: *My kingdom is not of this world* (John 18:36). With these words, Jesus drew a stark distinction between the kingdom He was inaugurating and the kingdoms of this world, which were based on power, violence, and control.

This statement, though seemingly evasive to Pilate, was not a denial of kingship but a revelation of a completely different kind of kingship—one that was not rooted in temporal authority but in the spiritual reign of God over the hearts and minds of individuals. Jesus made it clear that His kingdom was not concerned with overthrowing political systems or establishing an earthly empire. If His kingdom were of this world, His followers would fight to prevent His arrest. Yet, He was delivered up willingly, submitting to the authorities because His mission was far different from any earthly ruler.

Pilate, though intrigued, was also confused. *So you are a king?* (John 18:37) he pressed. Jesus answered, *You say that I am a king. For this purpose I was born and for this purpose I have come into the world—to bear witness to the truth* (John 18:37). Here, Jesus clarified His kingship was not about temporal power or political revolution. It was about revealing God's kingdom. His purpose was not to lead a rebellion but to speak truth to those who would listen, and to establish a new order—an order where the truth of God's love and justice would reign, not a kingdom of power or force.

The contrast could not have been clearer. Pilate, in his worldly perspective, found himself perplexed by Jesus' refusal to answer his questions directly or to defend Himself against the accusations of the Jewish leaders. Pilate saw Jesus as a pawn in a larger game, not understanding that the very "King" standing before him was the embodiment of the truth that could set the world free. Pilate, struggling with his own inner conflict and political pressures, ultimately sought to release Jesus but was thwarted by the cries of the crowd and the insistence of the Jewish authorities.

The Jewish leaders, too, misunderstood Jesus' mission. They were not seeking a spiritual king who would rule in the hearts of men; they wanted a messianic figure who would restore Israel to its former political glory. They saw Jesus as a threat to their power, influence, and control over the people. Their vision of the Messiah was one of military might and political victory, not the self-sacrificial servant that Jesus was. In their minds, it was better for one man to die than for the entire nation to be destroyed (John 11:50).

As Pilate attempted to navigate these conflicting demands, the power structures of both the Roman Empire and the Jewish religious system came into direct opposition with the radical nature of the kingdom Jesus was establishing. Pilate found no guilt in Jesus (John 19:4), yet he was manipulated by religious leaders and fickle crowds into condemning an innocent man to death. Pilate, desiring to avoid conflict, gave the decision to the crowd, who demanded Jesus' crucifixion. Even as he washed his hands of the responsibility (Matthew 27:24), Pilate knew the truth—he was complicit in condemning the very King who had come to establish a kingdom of peace.

"Before Pilate"

Before Pilate, Jesus stood,
A prisoner, condemned though good.
The crowd around Him cried for death,
Their shouts grew fierce with every breath.
"Are You a king?" the Roman asked,
His question veiled, his conscience masked.
But Jesus' eyes cut through the haze—
His kingdom not of earthly ways.
"My kingdom's not from realms below,"
He spoke of truth the proud won't know.
Not wealth, nor war, nor empire's claim,
But love and truth in heaven's name.
Pilate, caught in fear and doubt,
Could hear the truth, but not speak out.
He wavered in that crucial hour,
And yielded to the mob's dark power.
"Behold your King!" he cried in vain,
While mercy bowed beneath the strain.
Not with a crown men would endow,
But thorns upon His bleeding brow.
The crowd cried out, "Now crucify!"
A King condemned, the Truth to die.
Pilate washed his hands to cope,
But found no peace, no balm, no hope.
The silent Christ, so falsely tried,
Held heaven's power, though crucified.
No sword He drew, no throne He claimed—
Through sacrifice, His reign was named.
And Pilate, standing there alone,
Felt justice slip from bloodstained stone.
The King would reign, though not that day—
His kingdom not of this world's way.

Analysis

The exchange between Jesus and Pilate reveals the stark contrast between the kingdoms of this world and the spiritual kingdom that Jesus came to establish. Pilate, representing the Roman Empire, was focused on maintaining the status quo, where power, control, and military force were the measures of success. The Jewish authorities, on the other hand, were seeking a Messiah who would restore Israel's political power and independence. Jesus, however, came not to overthrow earthly powers but to inaugurate a kingdom that transcended political and military systems—one that was based on truth, love, and self-sacrifice.

Jesus' kingdom is not of this world—it is not built on violence or political ambition. His kingship is not defined by dominance or control, but by His willingness to lay down His life for the sake of others. In His dialogue with Pilate, Jesus made clear that His mission was not to engage in political battles but to reveal the truth that could set people free. Pilate's struggle reflects the tension between worldly authority and the radical nature of Jesus' spiritual reign. Ultimately, Pilate's failure to act on the truth led to the crucifixion, but it also set in motion the very fulfillment of Jesus' purpose—the establishment of His eternal kingdom.

Jesus resisted the expectations of both the religious and political authorities of His time, remaining faithful to God's purpose for His life, which was not to fulfill the popular messianic dreams of power and glory but to bring about a kingdom rooted in truth, service, and ultimate sacrifice.

Reflection

Pilate stood face to face with the Truth—and flinched. His role in the trial of Jesus is both historically significant and personally convicting. What would you have done in Pilate's place—when confronted by truth, but pressured by the crowd?

48

From the Cross

The sky had grown dark, and the earth trembled beneath the weight of the moment. The long-awaited day had come, and Jesus, the Son of God, was crucified. His hands and feet nailed to the cross, the crown of thorns pressed into His brow, He hung between heaven and earth—suspended in agony, yet fully aware.

The soldiers mocked, the crowds jeered, and those closest to Him wept. In this moment of unimaginable pain, Jesus spoke— words that echoed through the heavens and across time. Seven sayings, seven divine utterances, each revealing the depth of His love, the nature of His Kingdom, and the final victory over sin and death.

1. *"Father, forgive them, for they know not what they do."* **(Luke 23:34)** The first words from Jesus' lips were not words of condemnation, but of compassion. The very people who had mocked Him, beaten Him, and nailed Him to this tree were the ones He prayed for. *"Father, forgive them."* Jesus, in the midst of excruciating pain, extended grace to those who didn't understand the enormity of their actions. His forgiveness was not for those who deserved it, but for all who would come to Him in need of grace. These words revealed the heart of God—love that transcends even the deepest offenses.

2. *"Truly, I say to you, today you will be with me in Paradise."* **(Luke 23:43)** Next, He turned to the criminal beside Him, a man who had lived a life of sin, yet in his final moments found grace. The criminal had asked, *"Jesus, remember me when you come into your kingdom."* And Jesus, in His dying breaths, extended forgiveness and promised eternal life. *"Today you will be with me in*

Paradise." This statement demonstrated that salvation is not based on one's deeds but on the mercy of God. Even in His final hours, Jesus was still offering the hope of redemption.

3. "*Woman, behold your son… Behold your mother.*" (John 19:26 -27) As the Son of God hung on the cross, His thoughts were still on those He loved. He looked at His mother, Mary, standing at the foot of the cross, and then at the beloved disciple, John. *"Woman, behold your son... Behold your mother."* In this moment of agony, Jesus entrusted His mother into John's care, providing for her even in His final moments. His words spoke of love, familial responsibility, and care that transcended His own suffering.

4. "*My God, my God, why have you forsaken me?*" (Matthew 27:46; Mark 15:34) This cry cuts to the heart of the mystery of the cross—the anguish of the sin-bearer. Jesus, the Son of God, was not merely enduring physical pain; He was entering fully into the brokenness and alienation that sin brings. In the opening line of Psalm 22, a lament of David, He voiced both His suffering and the prophetic truth of the moment. In that cry, He expressed the deep sorrow of bearing the world's sin—not because the Father had abandoned Him, but because He was taking into Himself the darkness and guilt of sin. In this moment, He became the sin-bearer for all humanity, absorbing our estrangement so that we could be reconciled. His agony was not divine desertion, but redemptive love.

5. "*I thirst.*" (John 19:28) Jesus, in His humanity, expressed a simple yet profound need: *"I thirst."* He was not just thirsting for physical water, but His statement was symbolic of greater thirst—the longing for the fulfillment of God's redemption. The physical thirst He experienced reflected the deep spiritual thirst that only His death could satisfy. He, who offered living water to others, now hung on the cross in the agony of thirst, yet the living water quenching spiritual thirst would only be brought through death and resurrection.

6. "*It is finished.*" (John 19:30) With these words, Jesus declared the completion of the mission He had come to fulfill. *"It is finished."* The weight of sin, the curse of death, and the power of the enemy had all been conquered. Jesus had accomplished what He had set out to do—to reconcile humanity to God through His sacrifice. His death was not a defeat, but the ultimate victory. *"It is finished."* The work was done. The price had been paid. The Kingdom of God had come.

7. "*Father, into your hands I commit my spirit.*" (Luke 23:46) The final words of Jesus were words of surrender. After He had completed His work, He entrusted His spirit into the hands of His Father. *"Father, into your hands I commit my spirit."* Jesus, in His final act of obedience, surrendered His life to God, knowing that His death was not the end but the beginning of a new era. With these words, He entrusted Himself to the Father's will, knowing that the victory had been won, and the resurrection was about to unfold.

"The Sayings"

Upon the cross, the Savior spoke,
Words of life through suffering's smoke.
"Father, forgive"—a cry of grace,
For those who mocked His holy face.
"Today with Me you'll surely be,"
He said to one who dared believe.
"Behold your son," and "See your mother"—
Love entrusted to one another.
'My God, my God'—never alone,
As love bore guilt not once its own.
"I thirst," He spoke, with lips so dry—
Not just for drink, but Heaven's reply.
"It is finished," strong and clear,
The debt now paid, the end drawn near.

And then, "Into Your hands," He sighed,
The Son of Man hung down, and died.

Analysis

The seven sayings of Jesus from the cross open a window into the heart of His mission. Each word carries weight—revealing forgiveness, compassion, abandonment, fulfillment, and ultimate surrender. This was not simply a moment of death; it was the culmination of love.

Jesus began with forgiveness for His enemies and ended with trust in His Father. He spoke comfort to a thief, entrusted His mother to a friend, voiced the agony of becoming sin for those He came to redeem, declared His work finished, and gave His spirit into God's hands. These were not scattered cries but purposeful expressions that revealed His completed redemptive mission. The path to victory led through suffering—but in that suffering, Jesus revealed the depths of divine love.

Reflections

1. Jesus spoke words of forgiveness even as He was being crucified. How does His mercy challenge or inspire your own posture toward those who have wronged you?

2. One criminal responded with mockery, the other with faith. What do their different responses reveal about our ability to turn to Jesus—even in life's final moments?

3. Jesus' final words were of trust and surrender. Where in your life do you feel invited to say, *"Father, into Your hands I commit…"*?

49

A Cross for a Throne

As Jesus hung on the cross between two thieves, the world's expectations of a Messiah were brutally and visibly shattered. The idea of a mighty king reigning in power, wealth, and conquest was destroyed by a scandalous display of weakness and rejection.

A sign above Him read, "*Jesus of Nazareth, the King of the Jews.*" This was no accidental title. Pilate prepared a sign declaring the charge against Jesus, announcing His crime. But the sign, written in Hebrew, Latin, and Greek (John 19:19–22), was not so much a charge as it was a declaration. In the three dominant languages of the known world, the kingship of Jesus was proclaimed. It unintentionally echoed what the early church would soon boldly confess: that Jesus is Lord of all—Jew and Gentile alike.

Pilate might have meant it to mock the religious leaders or settle a score, but he ended up affirming something far more profound than he understood. "*What I have written, I have written*" (John 19:22) was not just political stubbornness—it was an unwitting confession. The sign declared royalty, while the crown was thorns, and the throne was a cross.

The Kingdom had come—but not as anyone expected.

Pilate's words unwittingly declared the true kingship of Jesus. Yet the very people who would have expected their king to overthrow Roman tyranny saw only a helpless man, condemned to death.

In the throes of His agony, Jesus' mission became even more apparent. As He forgave His executioners, He exemplified the power of grace in a world that expected justice to be served through strength and violence. Yet, even in the final moments, the contrasting views of the Messiah were unmistakably clear.

One of the thieves mocked Jesus, demanding He prove His kingship by saving them both. Railing and raging, his perception of greatness was one of power, control, and survival. In stark contrast, the other thief, acknowledging his own guilt and hopelessness, recognized Jesus as the true King. His plea, *Remember me when You come into Your kingdom*, was an act of faith that transcended the world's expectations.

The contrast could not be more stark. Even at death's door, the debate over expectations raged. Even here on the cross, Jesus went beyond expectations—one man got it; the other didn't. One man saw the possibility of paradise, the other saw only death, darkness, despair, and destruction. While one man railed, the other hailed, Jesus as His King.

Jesus responded with words that turned the entire concept of greatness on its head: *Truly, I say to you, today you will be with me in paradise.*

"The Penitent Thief"

A thief on a cross, with death as his fate,
Condemned for his sins, no hope to abate.
Beside him, the Savior, world in His grasp,
He turns with a plea—one final ask.
"Remember me, in Your Kingdom, Lord,
In Your fair justice, You will restore."
No words of reproach, no anger, no fight,
A cry for redemption in the fading light.
The Savior replied with mercy and grace,
"Today with Me, in a holy place."
Though Jesus would die and breathe His last,
The thief still lingered as time passed.
Who was he before, this man on the cross?
A life full of sin, yet not fully lost.

For in the final hour, grace found its way,
The thief found hope in the Light of day.
No time for good works, no path to perform,
Just faith in the One whose love could transform.
A simple plea, a soul confessed—
Mercy received, eternally blessed.

Analysis

The crucifixion of Jesus, between two thieves, is the pinnacle of divine irony—where the world's expectations of the Messiah's role are brought into stark contrast with the truth of His identity. As Jesus hung on the cross, His kingship was affirmed in a way no one could have expected: not by conquest, but by the ultimate act of humility and sacrifice. His throne was a cross, His crown of thorns, His scepter broken.

The two thieves, representing the divide between earthly ambition and spiritual truth, showcase the two paths of response to Jesus. One thief, consumed by despair and bitterness, saw only the failure of the Messiah to meet worldly expectations. Failing to recognize the truth of Jesus' mission and the meaning of His death, he rejected the possibility of redemption and died without hope.

The other thief, on the other hand, embraced the paradox of Jesus' kingship and, in his moment of ultimate vulnerability, acknowledged the truth of Jesus' innocence and sovereignty. His plea for mercy was a cry not of entitlement, but of humble faith.

This moment of redemption, offered to the penitent thief, underscores the radical nature of Jesus' kingdom. His rule was not of domination or rebellion, but of forgiveness and grace, available to all who recognize Him as Lord, even in His apparent weakness.

In this brief but profound encounter, we see the heart of the gospel: salvation is not achieved through power, but through the humble acceptance of God's mercy. Through this exchange, Jesus further defied expectations, demonstrating that His path to glory was through suffering, and that His kingdom was one where the least, the lost, and the broken are welcomed into paradise.

The cross was not only a place of death—it was a place of decision.

Reflections
Two men, equally condemned, responded to Jesus in radically different ways.
1. What does the contrast between the two thieves reveal about the heart's posture in recognizing truth?
2. Why do you think the penitent thief was able to see what so many others missed? What opened his eyes?
3. In what ways does Jesus' response to him challenge our assumptions about who is worthy of grace?

Journaling: A Cross, A Courtroom, A Cry
Take a moment to reflect on the scenes leading to this point: the false accusations, the silence before power, the cries from the cross. Each one reveals something about Jesus—and something about us.

Before *Pilate*, truth stood silent. Have you ever been afraid to act on what you knew was right?

At the *cross*, two thieves looked at the same Jesus. One railed. One believed. Which voice do you recognize in yourself today?

Write your own prayer, your own confession, or your own simple plea, like the thief's: "*Jesus, remember me...*"

50

A Mother's Grief

The scene at the cross is the pinnacle of Mary's emotional journey. From the angel's visit to the birth of her son, she had nurtured the hope of a promised Savior—one who would redeem Israel and bring salvation to the world. As a mother, she anticipated the joy of seeing her child grow in wisdom and favor, fulfilling His destiny as Messiah. Yet, in Golgotha's bleakness, Mary stands witness to the excruciating reality of the promise. She watches her son, Son of God, suffer in the most brutal way, His body broken, His life ebbing away.

Mary's pain was foretold by Simeon in the temple when he spoke of a sword piercing her soul (Luke 2:35). What began as a joy-filled journey in faith now culminates in a heart-wrenching moment of unbearable grief. The paradox of motherhood is felt deeply here—how could the promise of a Savior be intertwined with the agony of His death? How could the birth of the Redeemer mean so much pain for the one who bore Him?

Yet Mary does not abandon her son. She stays beneath the cross, enduring the loss of her son and the fulfillment of prophecy in the same breath. She knew the cost of this salvation, and as painful as it was, she chose to believe that this was the One who would bring redemption—not just for her, but for all of humanity.

The scene is filled with tension—the tension between hope and despair, the known and the unknown, the promise of God and the reality of suffering. The angel's message, *Let it be unto me*, echoes now in the silence of the cross, as Mary surrenders once again, this time not to a divine calling, but to the deep, incomprehensible sorrow of a mother who watches her son die.

"Beneath the Cross, a Mother's Heart"

She held Him first in trembling hands,
A child foretold by heaven's plans.
The angel's voice, the shepherds' song—
Could this be right? Could they be wrong?
She watched Him grow with wondering eyes,
A quiet boy, both kind and wise.
She pondered words too deep to know,
And let the years in silence flow.
At Cana's feast, she urged His grace,
She knew there dwelt a holy place.
But later came with kin and fear,
Unsure of what she'd come to hear.
She saw the crowds, the rising fame,
The whispered rumors of His name.
And yet, beneath the swelling tide,
She feared the world would turn aside.
And now, the cross. The nails. The cries.
The bruised and blood-stained sacrifice.
No throne, no crown but woven thorn,
A mother's soul by sorrow torn.
What thoughts returned within her mind—
The manger's light, the words divined?
What aching questions filled her chest
As thorns replaced His infant rest?
She could not reach. She could not save.
She stood in love before sure grave.
No protest made, no final plea—
Just silent faith, and mystery.
She saw the Son she could not keep,
And wept a loss for words too deep.
No voice from heaven, no angels near—
Just death, and blood, and every tear.

Yet even then, though hope seemed gone,
She stood. She stayed. She still held on.
For love remembers what it's heard,
And waits in silence for the Word.

Analysis:

The themes of Mary's grief at the cross are rich with biblical and theological depth, interwoven with the broader story of salvation and the fulfillment of prophecy. Mary's journey, from the announcement of the angel to the birth of the Savior and now to His crucifixion, reveals the heart of God's plan for redemption.

1. **Mary's Emotional Journey:** Mary's pain, while deeply personal, also carries theological significance. It fulfills the prophecy given by Simeon in the temple that a sword would pierce her own soul (Luke 2:35). This poignant prophecy highlights the tension of Mary's experience—she, who had given birth to the Savior, now watches His suffering unfold. Her emotional journey—from initial joy at His birth to anguish at His death—represents the complex nature of divine promises: they often come with immense sacrifice. The cross is the ultimate paradox of victory through suffering.

2. **The Reversal of Expectation:** Mary's grief is compounded by the reversal of her expectations. As a Jewish mother, she would have understood the promise of the Messiah in terms of triumph, power, and restoration. Yet Jesus' path is not one of earthly glory, but one of humility, rejection, and death. The title "Savior" takes on a different meaning when viewed through the lens of crucifixion. We are reminded God's ways are not always our ways. The Messiah would not conquer by force but through sacrificial love and death. The pain of the cross is paradoxically tied to the hope of redemption. God's kingdom often operates in reverse order to human expectations.

3. **Hope Amid Suffering:** Despite the profound grief Mary faces, there is an undercurrent of unwavering hope. Mary's faith, while

tested, remains rooted in the promises of God. She does not abandon Jesus at the cross; instead, she stands firm, enduring the sorrow, not because she understands it all, but because of the deep love she has for her Son. Theologically, this moment reflects the heart of Christian hope: the suffering of Jesus, though heartbreaking, is the very means by which humanity is saved. Just as Mary's love holds her at the cross, so too, Christian hope is held on the redemptive work of the crucified Christ.

4. The Cost of Salvation: Mary's experience at the cross is a powerful reminder that salvation came at a great cost, not just to Jesus but to those who loved Him. Mary's heartbreak reflects the agony of the Father's heart, who gave His Son for the salvation of the world. This personal loss underscores the universal cost of salvation. Jesus' death is the fulfillment of God's promise to bring redemption, but also the painful reality that salvation requires sacrifice. Mary's role as the mother of the Savior further emphasizes the magnitude of this sacrifice, as she both witnesses and participates in the cost of love.

Conclusion

Mary's grief beneath the cross embodies the paradox at the heart of redemption: salvation comes through suffering, glory through pain. The cross is the axis of history—where divine love meets human agony.

Reflections

1. Mary stayed beside Jesus in His suffering, though it broke her heart. What does Mary's faithfulness in grief teach you about how to love someone through pain?

2. Simeon told Mary a sword would pierce her soul. Have you ever felt tension between the promises of God and the pain of your present moment?

51

Sealed Against Heaven
Futility of Earthly Power Against God's Kingdom
(Matthew 27:62–66)

They sealed the tomb, thinking they could secure the silence.

The religious leaders feared more in Jesus' death than they ever had in His life. They remembered His words—*"After three days, I will rise."* Though they called Him an impostor, they couldn't shake the possibility that something might happen. Not because they believed—but because they didn't trust death alone to contain.

So, they approached Pilate on the Sabbath—the very day meant for rest—to request an act of control. *"Seal the tomb,"* they said. *"Post a guard. Stop the fraud."*

Pilate, wearied and indifferent, responded with one of the most ironic commands in Scripture:
"You have a guard of soldiers. Go, make it as secure as you can."

They tried.
They rolled the stone.
They set the watch.
They pressed the Roman seal into wax and onto stone, as if human hands could hold back Heaven.

But the Kingdom of God does not yield to caution tape and fear. And Jesus was not sleeping—He was dead. Stone cold. Lifeless.

Redemption had been purchased, but...without resurrection, it would remain unfinished.

The victory wasn't complete in the tomb—it would take the power of God to bring it to light.

The Power of God on Display

Romans 1:4 tells us that Jesus *"was declared to be the Son of God in power according to the Spirit of holiness by his resurrection from the dead."*

That moment was the proof. The divine stamp of approval.
In 1 Corinthians 15, Paul insists: *"If Christ has not been raised, your faith is futile."* The resurrection is not optional—it is essential.
The same was true throughout the early church's preaching.

- When Peter stood at Pentecost, his message was clear: *"God raised him up... we are all witnesses."* (Acts 2:24, 32)

- In Solomon's portico, after healing a lame man, he declared again: *"You killed the Author of life, but God raised him from the dead."* (Acts 3:15)

- When Peter spoke to Gentiles for the first time, the resurrection was at the center (Acts 10:40).

- When Paul preached in Pisidian Antioch, he said plainly: *"God raised him from the dead."* (Acts 13:30)

- And when he stood before kings, under accusation, he didn't retreat—he pressed the point: *"Why should any of you consider it incredible that God raises the dead?"* (Acts 26:8)

From Pentecost to prison, from Jerusalem to the ends of the earth, the resurrection was not a footnote to their message.

It was the message.

The ultimate validation. The fulfillment of prophecy.
The explosion of heaven's power into history.

The resurrection was, and still is, the watershed moment of human history. Not a metaphor. Not a symbol. A breaking-in of divine power that rendered all human opposition laughable and obsolete.

A Flash of Glory

The Gospels say nothing of what happened *inside* the tomb.

But some believe the linen shroud that wrapped Jesus' body—possibly preserved in what we now call the Shroud of Turin—holds a silent testimony. Not a relic to argue over, but a mystery to ponder.

If authentic, the image is not painted. Not dyed. It appears scorched—like a photographic negative, seared into the cloth by a sudden burst of radiant energy.

Some researchers have proposed that a powerful emission of ultraviolet radiation or other energetic particles emanated from the body at the moment of resurrection. This flash may have caused the linen fibers to oxidize and dehydrate, creating the characteristic yellow-brown image. Italian physicist Giulio Fanti has suggested that the image was burned into the uppermost layers of the cloth by a surge of "radiant energy"—perhaps ultraviolet light, X-rays, or even something beyond our current understanding.

What if, in that instant, the glory of God—the *effulgence*—blazed through death itself, and left its imprint not only on time and eternity…but on linen?

Much like the glory that surrounded Jesus at the Transfiguration, when His face shone like the sun. Not unlike the glory He prayed for in John 17: *"Father, glorify Me in Your presence with the glory I had with You before the world existed."*

If the image on the Shroud is real, it may well be the first and only photograph of resurrection glory—the moment when the Spirit of Holiness reanimated the dead body of the Son of God and shattered the grip of death forever.

The Seal Was Broken

The guards collapsed.

The seal shattered.

The stone rolled—not to let Jesus out, but to let the world *in*.

They tried to hold in the King of Glory with rocks and seals, but

Heaven was rising.

And in that empty space, where death once reigned, hope rushed in like morning light.

Jesus didn't escape—He was raised.

"You May Seal the Stone"

You may seal the stone and post your guard,
Call down your laws, stand ever on guard.
You may muster Rome with iron will,
But Heaven's breath cannot be still.

You may call Him fraud, impostor, threat,
Forget your peace, but not forget
The words He spoke with calmest breath:
"In three days' time, I'll rise from death."

So build your wall and set your seal,
Bind tight the tomb, deny what's real.
Yet watch, O world, with trembling fear—
For even sealed, the King draws near.

The stone will roll, the sky will blaze,
And death will lose its ancient claim.
You cannot hold what God will raise,
Or silence love by fear or shame.

So try your best to hold Him down—
The thorns, the cross, the Roman crown.
But come the dawn, the grave will fail,
And all of hell will turn pale.

For every seal and every sword
Still bows before the risen Lord.

Reflections

1. What does this passage reveal about how earthly powers attempt to control spiritual truth—and how they fail?

2. How does the resurrection of Jesus, performed *by the Spirit of holiness*, confirm His divine identity and secure your faith?

3. How might God's resurrection power be at work today in areas of your life that seem lifeless or sealed shut?

Journaling: Make It as Secure as You Can

Pilate's words still echo— *"Make it as secure as you can."*

What are the areas in your life where you've tried to seal off disappointment, bury pain, or protect yourself from despair as well as hope?

Where have you assumed that nothing more could happen—only to realize God was not yet finished?

Resurrection isn't just about what happened to Jesus. It's about what *has and can happen to us.*

Take a few moments to reflect on these questions in your journal: What parts of your life feel like a sealed tomb?

What "guards" have you posted to protect yourself from vulnerability, healing, or change?

What would it look like to invite the power of God's Spirit to roll away that stone?

Let the same Spirit who raised Jesus from the dead begin His work in you.

Prayer:
The God Who Breaks Seals, Risen Lord—
You saw the seals. The guards stood watch. You felt the cold of death—and still You rose.
The power that raised You cannot be rivaled, and no force on earth can hold back Your Kingdom.
I confess that I sometimes try to make things secure—I seal off what hurts. I bury what shames me. I post guards around my heart.
But You are the God who rolls stones away.
Come, Lord Jesus. Let Your resurrection power break through the dead places in my life. Let Your glory shine into the tombs I've sealed. Imprint Your image on me. Raise me to walk in newness of life.

I believe, Lord. And when my faith fails—help my unbelief.
And until the day when every tomb is empty and every tear is wiped away, I will trust You to finish what You've begun.

In Your risen name,
Amen.

52

The Eighth Sign
New Creation through Resurrection

In the Gospel of John, the seven signs perform an important role in revealing the identity of Jesus and the nature of His mission. These signs show His authority over creation, sickness, blindness, and death. But the final sign, the eighth sign, the resurrection of Jesus, is a sign in itself—a climactic event that inaugurates the new creation.

In John 11:1-43, the resurrection of Lazarus, the seventh sign that John chose, is the ultimate demonstration of Jesus' power over death, foreshadowing His own resurrection. Lazarus' resurrection, like all of the signs, also reveals the divine nature of Jesus and the Kingdom He brings. But it also points to something more— something that goes beyond the physical raising of a man from the dead. It points to the eternal, spiritual reality of new creation.

The resurrection of Jesus—His rising from the dead on the third day—is the true "eighth sign." In this act, God is not simply proving that He has power over death (Rms. 1:4), but that through Jesus, He is initiating a new order, a new heaven, and a new earth. The resurrection is the first fruit of this new creation, the beginning of the fulfillment of God's plan for the renewal of all things (1 Cor. 15:20).

This new creation is echoed in the final book of the Bible, Revelation, written by the apostle, John. In Revelation 21:1-5, the apostle describes a vision of the new heaven and new earth, where there will be no more pain, death, or suffering. God will dwell with His people, and all things will be made new. The resurrection of Jesus is the seed of this new creation, the foundation on which the restored world will be built.

The resurrection, then, is not just about personal salvation or the

victory over death; it is the harbinger of the total renewal of creation. Just as Jesus' resurrection led to the defeat of death and sin, it
signals the coming of a time when God will make all things new.
The new heaven and new earth are not just abstract concepts—they
are rooted in the power of Christ's resurrection, the first act of the
new creation.

"From Death to Life: Dawn of the New Creation"
From the grave He rose, a world reborn,
A light that shines on the darkest morn.
The first fruits of life, the first taste of grace,
In His resurrection, all things find their place.
No longer death reigns, no longer the night,
For the Light of the world has conquered the fight.
The old is gone, the new has come,
In the risen Christ, the victory is won.
A new heaven, a new earth, a new decree,
The Lion and Lamb, for all to see.
No more pain, no more strife,
Only the peace of eternal life.
And in that day, when all is made right,
We'll walk with our God, in the warmth of His light.
Resurrection is the promise, the seal, the sign,
Christ's new world, all made whole by love divine.

**Analysis: The Resurrection and the New Creation—The Ful-
fillment of God's Promise**
The resurrection of Jesus is more than just an isolated miracle—it is
the pivotal event in God's redemptive plan, the beginning of the new
creation that will one day encompass the entire universe. The resurrection of Christ is the first act of the new heaven and new earth,
which will ultimately be established by God. This concept of new
creation is central to the Gospel of John and the book of Revelation,

and it provides a powerful framework for understanding the significance of Jesus' resurrection.

1. **The First Fruits of the New Creation**—In 1 Corinthians 15:20, Paul calls Christ the *"first fruits of those who have fallen asleep,"* indicating that His resurrection is the beginning of the new creation. Jesus is the first to rise from the dead in this way, showing that death no longer has the final word. His resurrection is the foretaste of the resurrection that believers will experience in the future and the restoration of the created order. It is the first step toward the complete renewal of all things.

2. **The Fulfillment of God's Promise in Revelation**—The vision of the new heaven and new earth in Revelation 21 is the ultimate fulfillment of the hope that Jesus' resurrection represents. John sees a new world, free from sorrow, pain, and death, where God dwells with His people. This vision is the ultimate goal of the new creation that Jesus began with His resurrection. It is the world that God intends to create, where everything will be restored and made new.

3. **The Kingdom of God and the New Creation**—Jesus' resurrection also inaugurates the Kingdom of God, a kingdom that is not of this world, but is breaking in through the life, death, and resurrection of Jesus. The Kingdom of God is not merely a future hope but a present reality that began with Jesus' resurrection. Through resurrection, God demonstrated that the Kingdom of God is now among us, and it will ultimately be fulfilled in the new heaven and new earth.

4. **The Cosmic Scope of the Resurrection**—The resurrection of Jesus signifies that God's redemptive work is not limited to individuals alone; it extends to all of creation. In Romans 8:19-22, Paul speaks of creation itself groaning, awaiting the day when it will be set free from decay. The resurrection of Jesus is the beginning of this cosmic renewal, the first step toward the restoration of all

things. The new heaven and new earth are the culmination of this process, where God's glory will fill the entire creation.

5. The Call to Hope and Transformation—For believers, the resurrection of Jesus provides both hope and transformation. It is the assurance that death does not have the final say (1 Cor. 15:54-57), and it promises a future where all things will be made right. But it is also a call to live in the light of the new creation now. As followers of Christ, we are invited to be part of the restoration process, reflecting the hope of the resurrection in our lives and in the world around us. The resurrection is not only an event to be celebrated in the future, but a reality that should shape how we live today, as we anticipate the coming of the new heaven and new earth.

Jesus' victory over death was not only the personal hope for individuals but was the beginning of the ultimate restoration of all things, as promised in Revelation. It links the transformative power of Christ's resurrection to the future fulfillment of God's redemptive work in the world.

Reflections
1. How does understanding Jesus' resurrection as the "eighth sign" change the way you view Easter—not just as an event in the past, but as the beginning of something still unfolding? Why do you think the resurrection is the defining event for Christian faith and hope?

2. Revelation 21 promises a world made new—free from sorrow, pain, and death. In what ways do you long for that renewal, and how does Jesus' resurrection bring hope into those places?

3. If we are called to live now as part of the new creation, what might that look like in your daily life, relationships, or faith journey? How can the reality of resurrection reshape your perspective today?

53

Ascension
Promise of the Kingdom

The disciples stood together, watching as Jesus ascended into the sky. Their hearts were filled with wonder, confusion, and hope. For three years, they had followed Him, seen His miracles, heard His teachings, and witnessed His resurrection. But even at this pivotal moment, they still did not grasp what Jesus had come to establish.

As He was lifted up from their sight, their eyes remained fixed on the sky. The cloud that took Him out of their sight marked the end of His earthly presence. Yet, the silence of that moment was broken by the appearance of two radiant beings standing beside them.

These figures, clothed in white, spoke words that would echo in their hearts for years to come: *Men of Galilee, why do you stand looking into heaven? This Jesus, who was taken up from you into heaven, will come in the same way as you saw him go into heaven.*

The disciples had asked their question just before His ascension, still uncertain about the nature of His Kingdom: *Lord, will you at this time restore the kingdom to Israel?* They still hoped for political restoration—an overthrow of rulers and a visible reign of power. Their question revealed they had not yet grasped that Jesus' Kingdom was not of this world. It would not come with political might or military conquest, but through the powerful, invisible work of the Holy Spirit in the hearts of believers.

On that day, the Kingdom of God had not yet been fully realized. But the promise of the Spirit's indwelling, which would come at Pentecost, would change everything. The Kingdom of God is not territorial nor political. It is a spiritual reality—a people formed and united by the Spirit's power—across every nation, class, and culture.

The angels' words echoed the promise of Christ's return, His coming to establish His Kingdom fully and finally. The disciples would wait with expectancy, not for the immediate fulfillment they had anticipated, but for the *blessed hope* of His return. His absence would give way to the presence of the Holy Spirit, who would empower them to be witnesses to the ends of the earth, heralding the Kingdom that had begun in their hearts.

"Waiting with Expectancy"
The cloud ascends, and Jesus fades,
A moment hushed, the world still swayed.
"What kingdom now, O Lord?" they cried,
"Will Israel rise, be glorified?"
Two angels spoke in robes of light:
"Why gaze above, beyond your sight?
This Christ who left will come again,
In glory bright to rule and reign."
Not yet the throne, not yet the crown—
The Kingdom waits, not yet come down.
But in our hearts, His reign is near,
By Spirit's power, we persevere.
Our eyes now lift to heaven's door—
The King shall come, forevermore.
With hope we live, with grace we stand,
The Kingdom's call to every land.

Analysis
Acts 1 highlights two key themes central to the Kingdom of God:

1. The Disciples' Misunderstanding of and the Inauguration of the Kingdom
When the disciples asked, *Will you restore the kingdom to Israel at this time?*—they still envisioned a political reign, Israel would be the center of power and God's people would be free from Roman

oppression. The question focuses on last things, reflecting their expectation of God's final intervention to set all matters right.

However, it reveals their incomplete understanding of what Jesus had come to establish. Even after three years of following Him, they had yet to grasp the depth of His mission. Jesus' response—that it is not for them to know the times or seasons (1:7)—pointed to the mystery of God's timing. The full realization of the Kingdom would not come through their expectations of immediate restoration, but through a spiritual transformation initiated by the Holy Spirit.

This would be made clear on Pentecost, when the Holy Spirit descended and empowered the disciples to carry out the mission of the Kingdom. From that moment, the Kingdom of God would no longer be about a geographic location or a political entity, but about the spiritual reign of God in the hearts of believers. The church, as the Body of Christ, would be formed as a unified community of believers, irrespective of ethnic, social, or cultural boundaries.

2. The Promise of Jesus' Return

The words of the angels hold a powerful promise: *This Jesus, who was taken up from you into heaven, will come in the same way as you saw him go into heaven* (Acts 1:11). This declaration stands as a cornerstone of Christian eschatology (last things)—the Second Coming of Christ. Although the disciples expected Jesus to establish His Kingdom immediately, the angels reminded them that His ascension was not the end. It marked the beginning of the church's mission: to bear witness to the risen Lord, empowered by the Spirit and anchored in the hope of His return.

The Kingdom of God had already been inaugurated in the hearts of believers, but its final consummation would come when Jesus returns to earth in glory. The waiting the early disciples experienced is the same waiting we live in today. Christians are called to live with expectancy—the hope that Jesus will return, and that His Kingdom will be fully realized in the New Heaven and New Earth.

This teaching has profound implications for how we live in the present. We are called to live with anticipation and faithfulness, knowing that the full reality of God's Kingdom has not yet been realized, but will one day be. This hope compels us to live as citizens of the Kingdom now, working for justice, peace, and the spread of the gospel, even as we await the final revelation of the Kingdom.

Conclusion: Our Call to Live in Expectancy

The Ascension marks the moment when the visible reign of Jesus on earth transitioned into the invisible reign of the Holy Spirit in the hearts of believers. The Kingdom of God, inaugurated through Jesus' life, death, and resurrection, is now present in the hearts of those who believe. Fulfillment remains future, bound to Christ's return.

As we wait, we are not passive. Like the early disciples, we have been called to be witnesses to the ends of the earth, spreading the message of God's reign. And as we work and wait, we live with hope and expectancy, knowing that Jesus will return—just as He left, in glory and power. His return will bring the final establishment of the Kingdom of God, when He will make all things new, and His rule will be fully and forever realized (Rev. 11:15; 21:1-7).

The ascension of Jesus, the promise of the Spirit, and the hope of His return are all intertwined in the grand narrative of the Kingdom of God. As citizens of that Kingdom, we live in the tension between the "already" and the "not yet," faithfully anticipating the day when all will be made new.

Reflections

1. How does the disciples' question reveal the common confusion between earthly kingdoms and the Kingdom of God?
2. What does the Ascension teach us about the present reign of Christ and the role of the Holy Spirit in the life of the believer?
3. How does the promise of Christ's return shape the way you live today—as someone waiting, watching, and witnessing?

54

The Kingdom Fully Realized
The Reign of God and the Lamb

Throughout the Gospels, Jesus spoke often about the Kingdom of God—a Kingdom not of this world, a reign that would break in and change everything. From the moment Jesus began His ministry, He declared that the Kingdom had come near (Mark 1:15). His life, His words, and His miracles pointed to a world where God's will is perfectly done, where His reign is total and complete. But as we look to the end of the story—particularly in The Revelation—we see the fullness of what Jesus promised: the realized Kingdom of God, where God's reign is not hidden or partial, but fully established.

In Revelation 21:22-27, John paints a picture of the New Jerusalem, the place where God's eternal reign is realized in its fullness. There is no temple, no need for sun or moon, for the glory of God lights the city, and its lamp is none other than the Lamb of God, Jesus Christ. The nations will walk in the light of this divine glory, and the kings of the earth will bring their honor into the city, acknowledging the reign of the Lamb. There will be no night, and the gates of the city will never be closed—because there will be no more fear, no more enemies, no more sin. The Kingdom of God will be fully realized, and God will dwell with His people forever.

This Kingdom is not about a geographical realm; it is about the people of God, finally made pure and holy, living in perfect relationship with Him. In Revelation, we read that nothing impure will enter the city—only those whose names are written in the Lamb's book of life (Rev. 21:27). This final vision of the Kingdom shows the culmination of God's redemptive plan—a new creation: all things are made new; God's ultimate purpose for His people is fully realized.

Though God has always reigned as King over creation, the coming of Jesus marked the decisive inauguration of the Kingdom in a new and personal way—declared through His life, death, and resurrection. When we come to God by faith, we enter God's kingdom, that state where individuals seek His will in their lives. Yet, the fullness of that Kingdom will only be realized when He returns in glory.

The realized Kingdom is the end of the story—the place where God's reign is total, where His people live in perfect harmony with Him, and where all things are restored to their intended purpose. It is a Kingdom of perfect peace, justice, and joy. This vision, while still to come in its fullness, shapes the lives of believers today as we live with hope and anticipation, longing for that day when God's Kingdom will be fully realized.

"The Glory of God Among Us"

No temple stands in that holy place,
For God Himself fills every space.
The Lamb is the light, the flame divine,
And nations bow, His name to shine.
The gates of the city are open wide—
No darkness dwells, no sin to hide.
God's glory glows like blazing sun,
And in His light, all hearts are one.
The kings of earth their honors bring,
Their treasures laid before the King.
No night shall fall, no fear remain,
For God is near, and death is slain.
The streets are pure, the hearts made clean,
In God's own light, no shadow seen.
And only those the Lamb has named
Shall walk with Him, forever claimed.
This is the Kingdom, our heart's desire—

A world made new, set clean by fire.
Where all is healed, and all is right,
Where Christ the Lamb is endless light.

Analysis: The Realized Kingdom—God's Reign Unveiled:
The realized Kingdom of God is the culmination of all that God has promised throughout Scripture. From the Garden of Eden, where God's reign was first established over His creation, to the prophetic promises in the Old Testament about a coming Kingdom, to the teachings of Jesus in the Gospels, and finally to the vision of the New Jerusalem in Revelation, the story of God's Kingdom unfolds as the ultimate purpose of history. The Kingdom of God is not a distant ideal but a future reality that is inextricably tied to the person and work of Jesus Christ.

1. The Reign of God in the Present and Future: The Kingdom of God is both **already** and **not yet**. In the Gospels, Jesus declared that the Kingdom had come near in His ministry (Mark 1:15), and through His life, death, and resurrection, He inaugurated the Kingdom. Yet, the fullness of the Kingdom will only be realized when Christ returns. The tension between these two aspects—God's reign already present in the hearts of believers and yet to be fully established in the new creation—shapes the Christian life today. We live as citizens of God's Kingdom in a world marked by rebellion, awaiting the day when God's rule will be fully and completely realized.

2. The Presence of God in the New Jerusalem: In Revelation 21:22-23, we read that in the New Jerusalem, there is no temple, for the Lord God Almighty and the Lamb are the temple. This powerful image shows that God's presence will dwell fully with His people. In the Old Testament, the temple was the place where God's presence was uniquely located. The followers of Jesus are called God's temple (1 Corinthians 3:16-17; 1 Peter 2:5). But in the realized Kingdom, God Himself will be the source of light and life, and His presence will fill all things and all people (Revelation 21:3). There will be no need for the sun or moon, because God's glory will be the eternal light.

3. The Purification of God's People: One of the defining characteristics of the realized Kingdom is the purity of God's people. Revelation 21:27 tells us that only those whose names are written in the Lamb's book of life will enter the city. This underscores the importance of salvation through Jesus Christ's sacrifice for all sin for all time and the final purification of God's people. In the realized Kingdom, sin and death will be completely eradicated, and the people of God will live in perfect holiness and fellowship with Him. There will be no more tears, suffering, or sin; all will be made new.

4. The Fulfillment of the Kingdom's Purpose: The realized Kingdom is the final fulfillment of God's original intention for creation—to have a people who worship Him, love Him, and live under His reign. The imagery of the nations walking by the light of God's glory in Revelation 21:24 and the kings bringing their glory into the city (v. 24-26) speaks to the universal scope of God's Kingdom. His reign is not limited to a time, place, or people but encompasses all nations and all peoples. This proclaims the final reconciliation of all things to God, a harmony and peace spanning time and space.

5. The Eternal Hope of the Kingdom: For believers, the realized Kingdom of God is both a present hope and a future promise. While we experience the blessings of God's reign now—through the indwelling of the Holy Spirit and the advance of the Kingdom in the hearts of believers—our ultimate hope is for the day when Christ will return, and the Kingdom will be fully realized. On that day, God will make all things new, and His reign will be established forever. It is this hope that sustains us in the trials of this life and compels us to live as faithful citizens of the Kingdom today.

This brings our journey full circle, returning to the concept of the Kingdom of God and ending with the powerful and glorious vision of its realized fulfillment. By drawing from the imagery in Revelation and linking it to the hope Christians hold for the future, we are left with a vision of ultimate victory, peace, and restoration that is grounded in the promises of Scripture.

Reflections

1. Revelation describes a Kingdom with no temple, no sun or moon, and no closed gates. What do these images reveal about the nature of God's presence and reign in the realized Kingdom?

2. How does knowing that the Kingdom of God is both "already and not yet" shape the way you live today?

3. Revelation 21 tells us that only those written in the Lamb's book of life will enter the city. How does this promise inspire hope, and how does it call you to examine your own walk with God?

Journaling: Citizens of a Coming Kingdom

This final vision from Revelation brings our journey full circle. From the teachings of Jesus to the glimpses of glory ahead, we have explored the Kingdom of God as it breaks into the world—and now we behold it fully realized.

Use this space to reflect on the journey you've taken through these vignettes. Consider:

How has your understanding of the Kingdom of God changed or deepened?

Where have you seen God's reign breaking into your life as you've walked through this study?

What longings has this journey stirred in you for the final fulfillment of God's promises?

Take a few moments to write honestly and prayerfully. Record what you hope to carry forward as a citizen of the Kingdom—already present, not yet complete, but promised in glory.

55

Redeemed—Proclaim It

In the person of Jesus—the *Logos* incarnate, the Christ, the Anointed One—the cosmic drama of redemption was seen. The essence of the gospel is the heart of God. In the cross, God did for humanity what humanity could not do for itself—He made possible the restoration of relationship.

By His mercy and grace, we can become the children of God. We had a debt we could not pay—except by death. He paid a debt He did not owe—and by it we are redeemed. For all who experience His grace, we who are reconciled are given the ministry and the message of reconciliation. We are His ambassadors—the highest ranking representatives of one kingdom to another. Paul spoke of this in his version of the great commission:

Therefore, if anyone is in Christ, he is a new creation. The old has passed away; behold, the new has come. All this is from God, who through Christ reconciled us to himself and gave us the ministry of reconciliation; that is, in Christ God was reconciling the world to himself, not counting their trespasses against them, and entrusting to us the message of reconciliation. Therefore, we are ambassadors for Christ, God making his appeal through us. We implore you on behalf of Christ, be reconciled to God. For our sake he made him to be sin who knew no sin, so that in him we might become the righteousness of God (2 Cor. 5:17-21).

1. The Absence of Light and God's Omnipresence
The common interpretation that the darkness at the crucifixion reflects God's "absence" or withdrawal from His Son must be challenged. The idea that "God turned His face away" can sometimes present the notion that God, in His holiness, could not bear the sight

of Jesus' suffering. But the God who is omnipresent and who neither slumbers nor sleeps is not hindered by the absence of light. In fact, the darkness that descended on the earth from noon until 3:00 p.m. (Mark 15:33) was likely a supernatural sign—a manifestation of the profound spiritual reality that Jesus was bearing the weight of sin and the separation it causes between humanity and God. It was not a moment of abandonment from God, but a moment in which Jesus took upon Himself the reality of humanity's alienation from the Father. The cross was not about God "fleeing" from the Son, but about the Father and the Son together in the mission of redemption, even if the world could not understand it at that time.

2. Reconciliation in Christ (2 Cor. 5:16-21)

The passage from 2 Corinthians is, without question, one of the clearest and most powerful descriptions of the cosmic work of Christ's death. The idea that *God was in Christ reconciling the world to Himself* is a profound mystery and revelation. What we see in the crucifixion is not merely a man dying for his friends, but the Creator Himself, in the form of the Son, taking on the ultimate penalty for human sin.

This act of "self-reconciliation" is the very heart of the Gospel —the eternal *Logos* (the Word) made flesh, who chose to suffer and die to redeem what was lost. In doing so, He not only forgave us, but He also *reconciled* us, bringing us back into relationship with the Father. The phrase, *"not counting their trespasses against them,"* captures the heart of God's forgiveness. It is not a matter of ignoring sin, but of absorbing its cost and canceling the debt entirely. The cross represents the moment when God Himself paid the price for the rebellion of humanity, opening the door for us to become *the righteousness of God* in Christ.

3. Forgiveness as Absorption of Pain and Hurts

Dr. Ray Frank Robbins defined forgiveness: "Forgiveness is absorbing the pain and hurt done to you by another and then, treating that person as if they had never done it." This is an incredibly helpful framework for understanding the cross. When we reflect on Jesus' death, we must remember that God did not offer forgiveness merely as a theoretical abstraction. Forgiveness was achieved through the absorption of the pain, the hurt, and the consequence of sin—by God Himself.

This is what sets Christian forgiveness apart from human notions of forgiveness, which can sometimes be motivated by self-interest or mere tolerance. Christ's forgiveness was not a mere "passing over" of sin, but a costly act of taking on the sin of the world and its consequences. He, the sinless One, became the sin-bearer. *He who knew no sin became sin for us*—the ultimate exchange of justice and mercy. In this sense, the cross is the ultimate self-sacrifice—God absorbs our transgressions and forgives the unforgivable. In this, God is both just and the justifier (Romans 3:26).

4. The Cross as the Act of a Loving Father

The cross was not the moment when an angry God vented His wrath upon an innocent person. Too often, this view tends to create a dichotomy between the "wrath" of God and the "love" of God, as if God's justice and mercy are at odds with one another. But, it was in the cross that God's holiness, justice, love, and mercy converged in perfect harmony. God did not need to "satisfy" an angry impulse or "punish" His Son to make Himself feel better. Instead, He allowed Himself to bear the penalty that humanity deserved.

The Father, in His deep love, took upon Himself the burden of His creation's failure. The Father's will was not to have His Son suffer for the sake of some cosmic vendetta, but to fulfill the purpose of redemption—to bring salvation to the lost and to reconcile the world to Himself. The cross, then, is the supreme act of a loving Father who pays the ultimate price for His children.

5. The Cry of Sin's Absorption

The cry, *My God, my God, why have you forsaken me?*, is central to understanding the depth of Christ's suffering. In His humanity, Jesus expresses the utter pain and shame He experienced as He took on the sin of the world. But what makes this cry so powerful is that Jesus is quoting from Psalm 22, a messianic psalm that begins with feelings of abandonment but ultimately concludes with triumph and victory. While Jesus feels the weight of sin, He is not without hope. His cry is a moment of deep anguish but also a prophetic declaration of what would follow—the eventual triumph over sin and death.

What makes this moment so deeply moving is that in the cry of anguish, Jesus also expresses an *act of trust* in the Father. Even as He is made to feel the depths of our sin, separation, and rejection, He continues to reach out to the Father. His cry is a moment of brokenness, but it is also the moment when He *finishes* the work of atonement. He became in that moment our sin bearer. He became our sacrifice—our Atonement.

This paradox—the cry from the weight of sin and the act of redemptive love—is the heart of the Gospel. It is only through this moment of incomprehensible love that we can respond with worship and awe: *"Oh, the love that drew salvation's plan; Oh, the grace that brought it down to man."*

Conclusion

The crucifixion as the culmination of God's redemptive plan is both rich and profound. It emphasizes the self-sacrificial love of God and the mystery of the incarnation, death, and resurrection. The cross, in this view, is not a moment of cosmic anger, but the ultimate act of mercy, where God Himself absorbs the penalty for human sin and reconciles humanity to Himself. This act of forgiveness—absorbing the pain and hurt done by humanity, while offering restoration and reconciliation—is the heart of the Gospel.

The cross, in all its depth and complexity, remains the most beautiful paradox of our faith: it is both a moment of profound pain and the victory of love. It is through this moment that we come to know both the justice and mercy of God in the most intimate way possible.

"The Wounds of Love"
He who knew no sin, became our sin,
Bearing every wound the world would bring.
Upon His brow, the thorns did dig,
As Heaven watched the crimson sting.
The darkness fell, the earth did weep,
The Savior's cry was far too deep.
"My God, My God"—such despair?
Sin's full weight hung in the air.
"My God, My God"—never alone
As love bore guilt not once its own.
Yet in that cry, a victory sung,
The debt was paid, the battle won.
For love absorbed the cost of sin,
And broke the chains that bound us in.
O love so deep, O grace so wide,
That God would die, and death defied.
In suffering's grasp, our hearts were healed,
In perfect love, our wounds were sealed.
Now let us tell the story bright,
Of mercy born through darkest night.
For He, who died, now lives again—
His children now, not slaves, but kin.

Analysis:
The Great Commission—Bearing Witness to the Cross
The moment that Jesus proclaimed, *It is finished* (John 19:30), the veil was torn, and the way to God was opened once and for all. Yet, as we look at Luke 24:44-49, we see that Jesus did not leave His followers with a silent mandate to ponder His death and resurrection in isolation. Instead, He commissioned us to bear witness to this in-

credible message: that forgiveness, salvation, and reconciliation with God were now available to all through His work on the cross.

Jesus' commission in Luke 24:44-49 serves as a crucial moment in the story of redemption. It is not just a mandate for the disciples to go and preach, but a profound call to bear witness to the good news of the gospel—the message that Jesus died for our sins and rose again to bring us into right relationship with God. As Jesus explains to His disciples, the entire message of Scripture, from the Law to the Prophets to the Psalms, points to Him, the Messiah. He is the fulfillment of all that was promised, and His death and resurrection are the heart of the story.

Here, we see that our commission as believers is grounded in the reality of what Christ accomplished on the cross. His death for our sins was not simply an act of substitution—it was the ultimate act of reconciliation. Jesus bore our sin, but He also absorbed its cost. This is the message we are called to proclaim to the world—not just that Jesus lived, not just that He taught, but that He died for our sins, that He rose again, and that through Him, we can be forgiven and made new. This is the good news we proclaim.

The forgiveness offered at the cross is not just a theological abstraction or a concept to be debated; it is the foundation of our salvation and the message of hope to the world. As we bear witness, we are not simply telling the story of Jesus; we are sharing the very reality that through His sacrifice, all who repent and believe can be reconciled to God.

Bearing Witness to the Good News

The question that arises from this Great Commission is this: How do we, as the church, bear witness to this good news in a world that desperately needs to hear it? We are called to declare not only that God forgives but how He forgives. In Christ, God has absorbed the weight of our sin—the penalty we could not pay—and He offers us forgiveness as a gift. As we testify to this truth, we are not merely passing on information; we are inviting others into a life-changing encounter with God's love and mercy.

Our commission is not just preaching with words but living as witnesses to the transforming power of the cross. The world watches the church and the greatest testimony we can offer is a life that reflects the radical forgiveness we have received. We forgive as we have been forgiven; we love as we have been loved. In doing so, we make the message of the cross tangible to those who need it most.

The cross is the core of the gospel—the heart of our message. From this center our mission flows. When we bear witness to the death and resurrection of Jesus, we offer the world the gift of forgiveness. It is this gift that has the power to transform hearts and change lives, for it is the gift of God Himself. Through our witness, the world is invited to experience the depth of God's mercy and enter into the fullness of life He provided through His Son.

Conclusion

The beauty of the cross is that in the very moment of suffering and death, Jesus was accomplishing the most profound act of love the world has ever known. His death embodies God's redemptive love and forgiveness for the world. As those who have received this message, we are entrusted with the calling to bear witness to the cross— to tell the story of how God, in His great mercy, has reconciled the world to Himself.

In light of this, our mission is clear: we are to declare this good news to the world, to live as witnesses of God's mercy, and to invite others into the transformative power of Christ's forgiveness. Just as the disciples were commissioned to bear witness to the resurrection, we too are called to share the message of the cross, that all might come to know the depth of God's love and be reconciled to Him.

We do this not only with our words but with our lives—reflecting the forgiveness we have received and offering it to a world in desperate need of grace.

Get the companion to *Beyond Expectations*…

Profiles from Paul
A Life Poured Out for the Kingdom

What Jesus began, Paul explained and extended—through a Spirit -empowered life of mission, message, and ministry. *Profiles from Paul* explores the story of the early church through the eyes of the man who gave structure to the gospel and insight to the Kingdom. A devotional theology rooted in Acts and the Epistles.

In 75 short, reflective vignettes, the Apostle Paul's life is traced from conversion to calling, from mission to imprisonment. Each vignette includes biblical narrative, historical insight, original po-etry, and questions for personal or group reflection.

Written for everyday Christians, this book brings Paul's letters and legacy into focus with warmth, clarity, and conviction. Ideal for personal devotion, small group study, or leadership training, this resource invites readers to walk the path of faith with Paul as their guide.

Available at Amazon, Barnes & Noble, and retailers across the nation.

Also from the author:

It's NOT Adam's Fault!

A Decision in Carthage—
...over 1,600 years ago still shapes our world today... if you can believe it.

In *It's NOT Adam's Fault!*, the doctrine of inherited sin is questioned with clarity and conviction. What if sin isn't passed down, but is a personal choice? This book challenges "original sin" and offers a biblically grounded perspective on sin's true nature.

At the heart of this exploration is the Council of Carthage (418 AD), where the dogma of "original sin" was fused with infant baptism. What began as a theological decree became a power shift, used by the Roman Church to control monarchs, amass wealth, and dominate spiritual and temporal realms for centuries.

This wasn't just a doctrinal change—it was a historical turning point, one that reshaped Europe and beyond.

Through Scripture and church history, *It's NOT Adam's Fault!* reveals how a single, flawed translation altered Christian thought—and why Christ's freedom is far more radical and personal than we've been led to believe.

Are you ready to challenge what you've been taught about sin, salvation, and the gospel?

This perspective could change the way you see the world—and your place in it.

Available at Amazon, Barnes & Noble, and retailers across the nation.

www.ingramcontent.com/pod-product-compliance
Lightning Source LLC
Chambersburg PA
CBHW060052150626

46556CB00017BA/74